MARRYING

the Human Qualities
Needed to Marry Successfully

Don Burnard

First published in Australia in 2018
by Spectrum Publications Pty Ltd
a: PO Box 75, Richmond, Victoria, Australia 3121
t: (+61) 1300 540 736
f: (+61) 1300 540 737
e: spectrum@spectrumpublications.com.au
w: www.spectrumpublications.com.au
for Don Burnard

© 2018 Don Burnard
All rights reserved.
No part of this publication may be reproduced
in any manner without prior written permission of the publisher.
Cover Design: Tregraphic
Typesetting by Spectrum Publications Pty Ltd
Typeface: Bell MT & Helvetica

ISBN 978-0-86786-033-7

Images used with permission from the NSW State Archives:
NRS 12685, Sydney Harbour Bridge Photographic Albums 1923-33 items:
  Page 70 - 12685_a007_a00704_8728000190 View from Church of England
    Grammar School, Jul 1930
  Page 70 -12685_a007_a00704_8729000142 View from Bennelong, May 1930
  Page 71- 12685_a007_a00704_8730000050 Aerial View of Arch and Approaches
  Page 71 - 12685_a007_a00704_8731000008 View from Bennelong, Dec 1930
With Permission from Michael Moy:
  Page 72 - Sydney Harbour Bridge

A catalogue record for this book is available from the National Library of Australia

CONTENTS

Acknowledgements	v
Preface	vii
Introduction	1
Partners need to know the history and evolution of marriage	1
Early history of Marriage Education in Melbourne	2
What does it mean to marry?	6
Why the title of this book is 'Marrying'?	8
Describing marrying rather than defining marriage	9
An Action Plan for people marrying	9
From 'getting married' to marrying	10
From a static meaning of marriage to a dynamic meaning to marrying	11
From a pro-marriage culture to a pro-marrying culture	13
Four unhelpful cultures surrounding marriage	15
The Relatewell model (2000-2013)	21
A fresh approach to marrying – a new take on the life of couples	29
Life after Divorce	31
Everyone is born with the human capacity to marry successfully	32
Course Voting Process - Figure 1	34
Chapter 1: A shared meaning to marrying	36
The enduring values underpinning a meaningful pro marrying culture	40
Chapter 2: A strong 'self' is essential	44
What do we mean by 'self'?	45
4 Pillars Of Identity - Figure 2	46
The vitality of the self can be seen soon after birth	49
Leading an authentic life	49
The Self Tree - Figure 3	52
Chapter 3: Increasing our Self Valuing Quotient (SVQ)	53
Childhood and adolescence – learning to be a partner	56
Chapter 4: Valuing the differences between partners	60
Recognizing and adjusting to differences	61
A word of caution	62

Chapter 5: Being a bridge builder — 63
- The Sydney Harbour Bridge — 66
- A metaphor for bridge building between couples — 66
- Two-way traffic for both bridge-flow and marrying presents a similar challenge — 69
- The bridge construction - Figure 4 and Figure 5 — 70
- The bridge construction - Figure 6 and Figure 7 — 71
- The completed bridge - Figure 8 — 72

Chapter 6: Thinking, feeling and choosing — 73
- Some radical principles for managing feelings — 74
- Integrating thinking, feeling and choosing — 76

Chapter 7: A mature adult is always growing up — 80
- The centrality of interdependence — 82

Chapter 8: Taking our own needs and our partners needs seriously — 86
- Maslow's Hierarchy of Needs — 86
- Summarizing the five Levels of Need — 89
- Marrying is evolving – today more than ever — 90
- A brief history of people marrying — 90

Chapter 9: Integrating love and attraction — 92

Chapter 10: Communicating at a deeply personal level — 97
- The three channels of communication — 100

Chapter 11: Being a master of compromise — 103
- Challenging negative schemas — 105

Chapter 12: Enjoying our sexuality — 107
- Musturbators — 109
- Speaking about the unspeakable - sexual abuse — 111
- How does the sexual abuser operate? – recognizing the abuser — 111
- A good sexual relationship — 112
- An important question for a successful sex life — 112

Chapter 13: Understanding and monitoring our level of stress — 114
- Dealing with Stress — 115

Chapter 14: Carefully choosing our partner to marry — 119
- Both parties have a responsibility to carefully choose their future partner — 121

Three Important Readings Lists — 126

ACKNOWLEDGEMENTS

This book grew out of many hours spent listening to and working with couples and individuals who shared a dream that there is a vitality waiting to find expression in every human being.

Vision is one thing, translating it into reality is an enormous challenge. I could not have completed this task without the love and support of Brigid, my marrying partner of 31 years. As we continue to turn our marrying into both an adventure and a journey, I kept discovering the depth of her love and my love for her. Writing this book has helped me to respond more fully to her love.

I want to single out Laetitia (Letty) Gregory who edited my first book, *Towards a Life of Loving*, she convinced me to begin this second book and encouraged me to complete the task.

I want to acknowledge the message my mother Eileen, my father Harry and my sister Judy taught me that there are no short cuts to marrying successfully.

The mates who have been important in making my life productive and my relationships so valuable include the late Fred Rickard, John Ryan, Maurie Murphy, Ron Fitzgerald, John Nicholson and Frank Basile.

There were the women who welcomed me into their families and shared the delights of their children. There were also various orders of Nuns - they include the Brigidine Sisters, the Sisters of Charity, Faithful Companions of Jesus Sisters, Good Samaritan Sisters, the Loretto Sisters, the Sisters of Mercy, Presentation Sisters, Sion Sisters and other individual Nuns who assisted and supported the Pre-Cana courses from 1965 to 1980.

I also want to acknowledge the outstanding teachers in my life, Marist Brothers – Brother Ronald Fogarty, Brother Roger, Brother Romulus and De La Salle Brothers – Brother Stanislaus, Brother Oswald, Brother O'Day and Christian Brother Bill Greening. These were the finest men I ever met.

Finally, I want to acknowledge Val Noone who rescued me from the complexities and deadlines of editing and publishing.

PREFACE

This book is written for those who believe the most important choice they will make, or have already made, is their choice of a partner to marry. This involves understanding that although our desire to relate is innate, our ability to relate well is a learning process.

The psychological growth of each marrying partner, and of the children they may raise, is considered as both a goal and a responsibility.

The book is also written for psychiatrists, psychologists, social workers, adult educators and counsellors who seek an in-depth fresh approach to marital therapy, counselling and education.

I completed an Honours Degree in Psychology at Melbourne University in 1976. For fifty years I have spent most of my weekends working with couples and individuals in workshops of adult education for relationships. Over the same period, I have spent evenings both treating and counselling partners as a nationally registered psychologist. In those fifty years I have discovered that there are no experts in the area of relationships. On the positive side, I have evidence that more couples are moving from indifference, disillusionment, bitterness and failure to a more positive and reality based confidence to marry successfully and parent positively.

Marrying is not a question of finding the right person. It is about both partners becoming the best possible person while remaining true to themselves. It is not about measuring up to someone else's hopes and dreams. Furthermore, nothing causes the initial attraction to sour more than failed expectations, the fear of being different or the belief that there is only one right person.

Marrying functions best when two people encourage each other's growth. The need to grow intensifies as partners discover how different they really are. The challenge is for couples to discover that differences are the ore from which they mine the gold in themselves and in their relationships. The path to growth for both partners contrasts with their early spontaneous commitment to sharing interests, beliefs, values and chemistry. Romance, passion and infatuation are soon submerged as partners learn to live in a shared world rather than separate worlds. Intimacy can lead to a discovery that growth involves not only joy and excitement, but pain and disappointment.

To deal with the painful aspects of their marrying experience, both partners need to have a strong self and a growing capacity to self-value. This book gives significant attention to the much neglected subject of Self-valuing and the need to understand Self in a committed relationship. Choosing the right partner occupies an important place in this book. The distinction between attraction and love is made clear. It offers a strategy to avoid unnecessary heartache. The importance of really knowing and understanding one's prospective partner is emphasized.

No one knows what unexpected challenges lie ahead when people marry. The ability of both partners to deal with today's challenges is the safest grounds for believing they will be able to deal with whatever challenges tomorrow brings.

This book offers a new context which places the support of people marrying ahead of defending the Institution of Marriage.

A new hierarchy of skills are described. The first level skills are our human capacities to connect with our fellow human being without surrendering our uniqueness. These skills derive from the practice of kindness, justice, freedom, fidelity and honesty. These skills are reinforced by thinking freely, feeling deeply, enjoying simply and acting justly (choosing wisely).

Relationship skills are seen as being of second level importance. Third level skills include domestic chores and responsibilities.

All of these are self skills rather than ego skills and ego resources. They do not encourage comparisons and competitiveness. These three levels of skills enable partners to recognize more easily any power differential between them that undermines marrying. The most important skills in marrying are those which promote co-operation rather than competition. Everyone benefits no matter who actually develops the skills.

Qualities are much more than relationship skills or domestic skills. Qualities are forged by our experience as children, as teenages and as single men and women. Qualities that express our humanity unite us. Unlike achievements and skills, qualities create the stongest bonds within families and communities. Their secret is that they emphasize sharing and co-operation rather than competition. Happiness is not defined primarily by success. The greatest human qualities are those which help us recover from failure.

INTRODUCTION

Partners need to know the history and evolution of marriage

At the heart of the fierce determination of opponents to equal marriage rights was an ignorance of the constant evolution of marriage. This has occurred over centuries from the time humans first formed into tribes and gradually settled into societies with laws and culture.

In an *Age* newspaper leading article, Sociologist David Dawkins argued that marriage has always been an evolving reality. Family and marriage appeared about the same time in human history as agriculture began to develop. Before farming, people lived in hunter/gatherer communities.

There is evidence that wedlock has also been an evolving phenomenon since the earliest days of the human race. The earliest societies were built around a promiscuous matriarchal culture. Part of the evolution of what we know as marrying has been due to the transition in society from foraging to farming and then from farming to the industrial revolution.

Today the achievements of the industrial revolution are being transformed by Information Technology. The evolution of marriage has been rapid and dramatic whenever there is a significant cultural or economic shift in civilizations. Today we are witnessing a profound change in marriage rituals and arrangements due to the Information Technology Revolution. The Industrial Revolution had crushed families into row after row of tiny homes to create a bountiful source of labour for the satanic mills. The greatest change in marrying in the last 40 years has followed the Family Law Act passed in 1975 by the Labour Government under Prime Minister Gough Whitlam.

It is more important to keep marrying than to stay married. Marrying needs to be redefined as an ongoing journey and adventure. Most of 'getting married' is a prosaic ritual not able to reflect the depth involved in the challenges of marrying. The word marrying emphasizes that the focus needs to be on the couple and their growth, not just for the memorable features of the wedding day. The idea that we can 'get married' is heavy with expectations, fantasy and obligations.

Marrying requires an apprenticeship stage that enables couples to practise the many skills involved in marrying. Success in marrying depends on the couple, their choice of partner and life style, not so much on the memorable features of the wedding, the venue or the speeches, etc.

Marrying acknowledges two distinct developmental phases. The first is a practical apprenticeship which begins the process of marrying. The second is a continuing education process for the duration of their marrying.

Early history of Marriage Education in Melbourne

The first marriage education courses in Melbourne were both Church-based and secular courses. The Young Christian Workers (YCW) was a radical youth movement within the Catholic Church founded by Joseph Cardijn in Brussels in 1912. Cardijn was a Cardinal who recognized that Christian Churches were losing contact with youth, especially those who had very little education. The movement included young people from all walks of life. Its aim was to empower them to take positive action in their lives and community. Following its first World Council in Rome, Italy in 1957 it became an international movement. Priests were encouraged to move out of their presbyteries to get closer to the working class and prevent them drifting away from the church. The conservatives in the Melbourne Catholic Church in the 1960s were alarmed by the YCW movement and saw it as a form of Communist infiltration.

In 1962 Pope Paul VI rejected the Second Vatican Council's 'Yes' vote which would have allowed couples to use the contraceptive pill to plan their family size. Conservatives in the Melbourne Catholic Church, in particular the Anti-Communist forces loyal to B A Santamaria, began to campaign for a return to orthodoxy in the Melbourne Catholic Church and its many programmes.

I was ordained as a Catholic priest in 1960. In August 1965 I was appointed Chaplain to the Pre-Cana movement. (Cana was a town where Jesus had attended a wedding ceremony). I set out to increase the number of engaged couples attending Pre-Cana courses. I was advised by a wise older priest to spend twelve months observing the courses, their content and their approach before making any changes. This I did, and in the ten years from 1965 to 1975 with my suggested changes the numbers attending the Pre Cana courses increased from 400 couples to over 1,800 couples. A major influence on the pre-marriage courses had been the writer Ivan Illich. His works include *Deschooling Society* (1970), *Energy & Equity* (1973) and *Disabling Professions* (1977).

At about this time other denominations began establishing pre-marriage courses. In the 1970s John Robson, the Director of Interrelate in Sydney and myself succeeded in obtaining funding from the Federal Government to run pre-marriage education courses. At this time conservative forces in the Catholic Church came to believe that the Pre-Cana movement was becoming less orthodox in advocating the Papal teaching on the contraceptive pill. Significant changes were taking place in the pre-marriage programmes. As Catholics were becoming better educated and schools were encouraging students to think for themselves, sponsorship by the Young Christian Workers movement was becoming less relevant and influential. Meanwhile the identity of the Pre-Cana movement was changing. The name 'Pre-Cana' was abandoned and courses were renamed Pre-Marriage Education. The process was shifting to an adult education framework. The experience of the couples needed to be the focus and the source of change rather than the church's teachings.

While I remained under extreme pressure to teach the Catholic Church's orthodoxy, at the same time complaints to the Archdiocese of Melbourne about the content of the course increased. It appeared that there was no room for me as an Adult Educator or the participants of the courses to question Papal teaching. I then received a letter from the Vicar General of the Melbourne Catholic Church stating that my priestly income would no longer be paid by the Church. John Robson and I had argued successfully for a Government grant to create a culture that would encourage a serious commitment to pre-marriage education among couples planning to marry. The Chancellor of the Catholic Archdiocese, Penn Jones, informed me that my priestly salary would now be taken out of the new Federal Government funding. I was bitterly disappointed that the Government funding should be used to pay my salary rather than improving the quality of pre-marriage courses at the newly formed Marriage Education Institute Inc (MEI).

The Chairman of the MEI, Dr Ron Fitzgerald, pointed out that as a registered psychologist and as the MEI's Director, I could earn, in one day's work, the equivalent of my weekly priestly stipend. He wrote to the Chancellor telling him that in line with his direction, the Director's stipend would be met from other available funds. I succeeded in gaining employment as a psychologist at the Queen Victoria Hospital. The Catholic Church did not have to pay a cent to keep the MEI engaged couples courses going. I made sure of that by using part of my hospital pay. Meanwhile, the church set about establishing a number of alternative Catholic pre-marriage courses. That reduced the pressure on MEI courses to meet the church's demands on course content. Three major and positive outcomes emerged from this new freedom. The first was the change from the name Marriage Education Institute (MEI) to the Family Relationships Institute (FRI). The second was the use of the name Relatewell which I registered as a business under my name. The third was the instigation of a planning committee which included Ron Fitzgerald, one lawyer, three psychologists, two medical specialists and two businessmen.

The Family Relationships Institute is now an independent Non Government Organization (NGO) founded in 1978 by myself and Ron Fitzgerald. Interrelate and FRI were two of the earliest bodies to be funded by the Commonwealth Government to provide marriage education courses following the new *Family Law Act* of 1975. Within ten years most organizations found there was a falloff in the demand for marriage courses and they diverted most of their funding to marriage counselling. The shift from dissecting relationship skills to exploring what particular experiences mean to each partner proved invaluable. Relatewell refers to the Institute's varied adult education courses of marriage education which I designed while Director of FRI.

The number of people attending Relatewell's professionally based courses promoting people's ability to marry successfully has remained stable. More importantly the response of participants to these courses has deepened. The change in the couples' level of motivation and enthusiasm for various course activities has been dramatic. As the control for the course process was given to the participants, the years 2000–2013 were characterized by increased co-operation, commitment and sharing from the course participants.

Marrying: the human qualities needed to marry successfully has been written to ensure a renewed commitment to the Relatewell model and its ability to motivate couples to discover within themselves and their experiences a pathway to marrying successfully.

What does it mean to marry?

Peoples' questions about marrying are increasingly about meaning. What does it mean to marry? What does it mean to love someone? What does it mean to be loved? What does it mean to be a partner? What does it mean to be a parent? Who has the most influence in the lives of our children? People don't want smart answers or ideology.

Nothing epitomizes the search for meaning more than marrying. People need action plans with realistic goals. They also want to design together a unique style of marrying in which each partner is able to express their unique personality.

The division between home and workplace is less defined. In an age of mass information, constant talk and commentary without conviction, is anyone listening? Is anyone taking a stand? This book attempts to find a pathway through these issues by raising the important questions and discovering what promotes the best avenues of growth for those marrying. What underlies all these questions is a search for meaning.

This book draws inspiration from the Women's Liberation Movement. The founders of this movement argued that Women's Liberation had to be synonymous with the liberation of mankind generally. Men need to liberate themselves as women are learning to do. In particular, men need to liberate themselves from the belief that physical size and financial advantage entitles them to power and authority over their partners and their children.

Marrying has meaning when it enables partners to express their uniqueness through intimacy with each other. Partners need to keep constructing a dynamic meaning to self, to our differences, to love, to sexuality, to family, to society and to our world as a global village. Marrying does not require partners to have an identical meaning. Rather, it requires partners to share their distinctive meanings.

A case for marrying must be psychologically based, authenticated by the experiences of those choosing to marry and contributing to the growth of each partner and every child in the family.

Marrying has two dimensions. The first is the relationship between the two adult partners; the second is the family dimension if and when these adults take on the responsibility of raising children to take a constructive role as adults in society.

The biggest threat to marrying successfully is that so many children lack a positive role model of what it means to marry.

To explore marriage primarily as a legal or religious concept is not the scope of this book. Rather, the purpose is to recognize the actions, thinking patterns and emotional expressiveness which will decide whether their lives as partners will expand through understanding and commitment, or drift into alienation and misery. Will couples get on with the challenge of marrying or stay together for appearances sake?

Why the title of this book is 'Marrying'?

Between 1965 and 2013 I spent most of my weekends working with groups of couples planning to marry. Three nights each week I spent time working with couples planning to divorce. When I began working with couples planning to marry, the current wisdom was to avoid divorce by letting couples know the pit falls that lay ahead. This approach drew little response from couples who were experiencing a strong attraction to each other and who believed they could continue to cope well with whatever difficulties life might throw up in their paths. The difficulty is that marrying as an intimate connection, presents couples with challenges that cannot be anticipated. There are so many issues that lie beneath the conscious surface.

A new psychological approach was needed. This was partly provided for me by John M Gottman, *The Seven Principles for Making Marriage Work (1999)* and *The Marriage Clinic, A Scientifically Based Marital Therapy (1999)*. Another author who made an impact was David Schnarch, *Passionate Marriage (1997)*. Despite the positivity of these new initiatives, there has been little change in attitudes towards helping people recognize the key performance indicators (KPI) for success in marrying.

To me, the problem is the word 'marriage'. I believe it is much easier to build a positive narrative around marrying than it is to build one around marriage. What is needed is a new narrative which focuses on achieving outcomes that touch the soul of those trying to marry.

We need to replace an allegiance to the institution of marriage with an allegiance to the growth of both partners. This would involve a culture of continuing adult education. In this context, Marrying would focus on strengthening our identity rather than enhancing our reputation?

INTRODUCTION

Describing marrying rather than defining marriage

The challenge for all of us is to work towards an agreed description of marrying that is inclusive. The time has come to switch the emphasis from rancorous debate about the pros and cons of marriage as an institution to a rigorous exploration of the marrying behaviours that will enable partners to thrive rather than just survive.

Two themes keep recurring in philosophy, psychology, theology, literature, drama and cinema:

1. Marriage, as an institution, is in crisis.

2. The most secure basis for establishing a positive, stable and nurturing family life is a committed, intimate, loyal and mutually supportive and egalitarian relationship between the two adult partners.

An Action Plan for people marrying

This needs to be translated into an action plan. *A loyal and egalitarian commitment by two adult partners to mutual sharing and support of each other through good times and bad. The goal is striving towards physical, mental and emotional intimacy as the firmest base for positive and stable family life.*

In choosing to adopt the verb 'marrying' rather than the abstract noun 'marriage', adverbial phrases such as 'being married' or passive phrases such as 'getting married', I hope to foster a fresh dialogue about marrying and raising a family. This approach will shift the emphasis from defending marriage to exploring how a dynamic approach to committed partnering can become a psychologically rich life style.

Culture is a critical component of whether a civilization flourishes or collapses. A culture requires improvement of the mind by drawing people into the collective wisdom of our current times and times past. Growth of a culture is an organic process rather than a manipulation by modern mass media or a misuse of authority.

From 'getting married' to marrying

As an Institution, marriage needs to divest itself of any remaining hues of patriarchy and paternalism. Marrying needs to enshrine the best personal qualities of human interaction. There are many ways of marrying successfully as there are people marrying.

By contrast there is only one way to get married. That is by making vows in the presence of an authorized Marriage Celebrant and ending up wedded. There are a host of rituals, traditions, customs and formalities associated with the wedding. The skills involved in arranging the wedding and its associated paraphernalia are quite distinct from the human skills required to settle down and adjust to marrying. The title for this book was deliberately chosen to redress the imbalance between the verb marrying, which is a doing word, and getting married, which is more an isolated event, or the state of marriage as an acknowledged way of life.

Marrying needs to be recognized as a mature art and skill and to be redefined as an ongoing journey and adventure.

Most of 'getting married' is by contrast a prosaic ritual lacking the depth involved in the challenges of marrying. The word **marrying** emphasizes that the focus needs to be on the couple and their growth, not just for the memorable features of the wedding day. The idea that we can 'get married' is heavy with expectations, fantasy and obligations.

Marrying needs an apprenticeship stage that enables couples to practice the skills for marring. Success in marrying depends on the couple, their choice of partner and life style. The memorable features of the wedding may soon be forgotten as reality takes over.

Marrying on the other hand acknowledges two distinct developmental phases. The first is a practical apprenticeship which begins the process of marrying and the second is a continuing education process for the duration of their marrying.

This is not an argument for dismantling the Institution of Marriage. It raises the question of whether the best way to support people marrying would be less emphasis on the wedding and associated events and more emphasis on the personal growth of the partners choosing to marry.

Would it be more useful to encourage couples to prepare themselves psychologically through adult education programmes? Relatewell has provided such programmes with growing success for at least twenty years. The years 2000 – 2013 had been the most successful.

From a static meaning of marriage to a dynamic meaning of marrying

How long has marriage existed? In its present shape not very long. Scholars believe marriage was contemporaneous with the establishment of agriculture and the settling down of people to farming. What we now know is that marriage has undergone profound change as it progressed from guaranteeing survival for the small tribe to maintaining property rights to contributing to social order.

Since marrying has continued to pass through different stages. The biggest change in marrying in the last 80 years has been the scientific development of safe and effective contraceptives. Both partners are able to contribute to a less stressful and anxious life style if they wanted smaller families. Women are able to return to their careers relieving financial stress on families when there was only a single provider. Partners now need to work harder to become best friends and avoid drifting apart. People are living longer due to improved health measures. The finest human qualities are now more important than ever to marry successfully. They are idiosyncratic and therefore don't lend themselves to comparisons.

Reading about the different ways people marry successfully is always interesting and informative for two reasons. There is no one way of marrying that is right for everybody. On the other hand, there are ways of marrying that can diminish one or both partners and harm children psychologically. The focus of this book is not an abstract noun called marriage.

This book promotes ways of marrying which enable both partners and each of their children to keep growing up. Marriage is such an emotionally charged word. As an abstract noun it lends itself to endless theorizing and debate.

The reason there is such a passionate anti marriage camp on one side and an equally passionate pro marriage camp on the other side is that neither side listens to the others experiences in marrying. The gulf between pro and anti-marriage camps grows out of the fact that as children and adolescents people have such contradictory experiences in marriages.

Anti-marriage proponents point to marriage as often being the last bastion of patriarchal power, a licence for the continuing domination of women and the emotional mental, physical and, at times, sexual abuse of children. Pro marriage proponents argue that despite these too common violations, marriage remains the choice of a majority of men and women across diverse cultures and age old traditions. They still believe that marriage can be an oasis of tenderness and an impregnable fortress against a heartless world. Neither of these two philosophies provide a firm enough basis for understanding what it takes to marry successfully.

From a pro-marriage culture to a pro-marrying culture

The goal is to establish a pro **marrying** culture within our society. It is important to replace the pro marriage culture which fosters intransigent view points and safeguards property rights for those who can afford the best legal support. The word marrying switches the emphasis on to the verb to marry rather than gaining membership of the institution called marriage. Marrying exists for the wellbeing of people rather than to force people to subscribe to the institution of marriage.

As a psychologist and facilitator in adult education, my constant pursuit has been to find a meaning to marrying. This search began with my first book *Towards a Life of Loving (1975)*, Hill of Content. Other books which have influenced my thinking are:

- Viktor Frankl, *Man's Search for Meaning* (1959), *The Doctor of the Soul (1955) and, Psychotherapy and Existentialism (1967)*;
- Abraham Maslow, *A Theory of Human Motivation* (1943), covering his work on the *Hierarchy of Needs*; and
- Robert Kegan, *The Evolving Self (1982) and In Over Our Heads (1994)*.

In 1978 I founded the Family Relationships Institute (FRI) with the goal of searching out a shared meaning to marrying. The fundamental principle underlying this organization was that marrying and raising a family were best supported by the personal qualities of the partners, not just the practical challenge of providing material security for every member and the skills to relate well.

The next most powerful influence that inspired the writing of this book has been the hundreds of couples who were given a voice at the Institutes Relatewell Workshops. They responded positively to the opportunity to process their own experiences.

This contrasted with their lack of response to content. When the process touched their experiences in the NOW of their relationship they became motivated to participate.

Much of the content in this book has been developed by participants who believed they were being listened to. Emphasizing the content of experts may make participants sit up and take notice, however it doesn't achieve active learning. It doesn't motivate participants to actually challenge their thinking, adapt their behaviour or express their needs.

Marrying needs to find a meaning in a post-modernist world which constantly questions fixed beliefs. This includes meanings set in stone and purposes defined by powerful elites. Over the years I have sought to discover a meaning to marriage that has been enriched by the challenge of post-modernist thinking so well expressed in the writings of Jean-Francois Lyotard, *The Postmodern Condition: A Report on Knowledge (1979)*. Postmodernist thought cannot be ignored. Can marrying have a meaning in a world which challenges the core of all the institutions of society. Culture constantly impacts on art, literature, cinema, theatre, politics and economics. Who can stop it impacting on marrying and the family?

For the post modernists, meaning is constructed. There is no outside authority to finally determine meaning. For Lyotard, meaning is not discovered, it is constructed, crystalized and validated in peoples' experiences. Meaning is constantly being constructed and therefore constantly changing. Family life has become more challenging as society becomes more complex and continues to rapidly evolve in the digital age. The family is becoming less and less a safe haven. Poverty is breaking out amongst the lower middle classes. The richest nations are fighting wars in the backyards of smaller sovereign states – Afghanistan, Iraq, Syria, Lebanon and Palestine. The role of the family is increasingly needed to provide greater emotional security through stable, positive and loyal relationships.

Four unhelpful cultures surrounding marriage

If we surround marrying with pious platitudes, pop psychology, unachievable dreams and expensive frivolities, we may continue to seduce people into getting married. Society needs to create a culture which reminds us that although it may be easy to get married, to marry is the biggest challenge life offers us. It is only possible to do this if we understand what it means to be an adult - and that we need to keep growing up right throughout our lives. To think marrying is easy may not just lead to a tender trap, but to a vicious circle of disappointment and disillusionment in which everything turns out not to be easy but increasingly difficult. There are plenty of people who do not want to marry. They don't need our pity. They will be content to face death surrounded by their true loyal friends. The problem with marriage lies in the cultures surrounding it. Four themes stand out as significantly unhelpful to those wanting to get on with marrying:

- The Dream Culture.
- The Traditional Culture.
- The Commercial Culture.
- The Legal Culture.

These four cultures are focused on the institution of marriage rather than the people marrying. They do little to support partners in their search for a meaning to marrying. It is not their focus to promote the personal growth and maturity of those who plan to marry. Part of the problem is that none of these cultures are created by the partners marrying. Couples are swept up in these cultures. Let's explore these unhelpful cultures.

1. The Dream Culture

From an early age, generations of children have been told that this is what life holds out for you. "When you have grown up, you will meet the person who is right for you, you will fall in love, you will get married, have children of your own and then your children will follow suit." This is a fable, a reassuring story not based on fact. Let's take this fable apart step by step:

- *"When you have grown up"*

    Reality: Growing up is a lifelong process. The day we stop growing up we are on the way to becoming a boring partner. Too many people are psychologically dead by the time they reach 21 years of age. It is an increasing problem which I encounter in my work as a psychologist. Psychological death is characterized by making no new friends, developing no new interests, no new ideas, taking no new responsibilities and constantly trying to solve problems with old strategies that have not worked.

    The Dream Culture gives little meaning to the challenges involved in puberty which begins the transition to responsible adulthood. It ignores the challenges of puberty which are characterized by embarrassing growth spurts for some and painfully anxious delays for others. Puberty can strengthen the confusion that size, power and popularity seem to be the best prizes in life. There are so many distractions to stop adolescents from developing their capacities to feel deeply, enjoy simply and choose wisely.

    Marrying involves two **growing-ups** rather than two grown-ups. Growing up, as a lifelong process, is not an automatic process like physical secondary sex characteristics.

- *"You will meet the person who is right for you"*

    Reality: We don't just meet the right person. Each partner needs to help create the right person. If there is one right person there are probably hundreds more you could meet in your life time. The challenge for each partner is for they themselves to become that right sort of person, not find one.

- *"You will fall in love"*

    Reality: To believe we can fall in love is to surrender ourselves to a biological force of nature. That biological force is attraction between people. Who can forget their first experience of being swept off their feet by someone they have just met or seen from a distance? These first attractions indicate that we are ready to leave childhood with its security. We are becoming less centered on dependence on our parents and our once important toys. We are beginning to recognize the possibilities of a richer life through closeness to another person of my choice. The stronger the attraction, the more possibilities I may expect from the relationship. To fall for another person is to switch dependencies from parents to a new significant peer. Chapter 12 will explore the reason attraction is an inadequate basis for making the most important choice we will ever make in life – my marrying partner.

- *"You will get married"*

    Reality: To **marry** is a verb. Marrying is an action I choose. It is not something done to me. Marrying gives us the chance to love each other in so many different ways. The phrase 'get married' is language pollution at its worst. We can get wedded in a ceremony and emerge with a marriage certificate. We can get robbed, get sick and get over it but we cannot get married. People who play golf never describe their experience as **getting golfed**.

I can't marry on my own. I need a partner who is as committed to marrying me as I am to marrying my partner. The reality is that any day one of us stops marrying, then we are not "married" for that period. This fact is difficult for us to comprehend as long as we believe we can get married. Marrying is more than being incorporated into the institution of marriage. Marrying is something both partners need to do. It is not something that is done to them. The wedding ceremony and the marriage certificate are a statement of intent. The most we can do is use each day to marry, secure in the knowledge that both of us are serious in our intent to share our lives in a variety of ways.

- **"You will have a family with children of your own"**

    Reality: We can have many things in life. We can have a headache. We can have disappointment. The reality is that we don't just have a family, we need to build a family and it is both an exhausting and fulfilling task.

- **"And you will live happily ever after"**

    Reality: Marrying, like happiness, is not a blissful destination we arrive at. It is a way of travelling through life. There are moments of intimacy and joy. But, we remain very different individuals and can still experience a sense of loneliness and even isolation at times.

2. The Traditional Culture

There can be a problem in cross cultural weddings. It may be important for parents and grandparents to retain the tribal traditions within their culture on such significant occasions as giving birth, marrying and dying. Many of these practices can prove extremely costly, involving extended family and even people from the same village back in Europe, Africa or the Middle East. There can be a clash of values, especially if the younger generation have adopted the more materialistic focus of owning their own home and postponing starting a family until they are out of debt. What is the point of continuing to live immersed in a culture they have left? Both partners need to take a part in building a place in a culture that may be new for both of them. Part of the traditional culture was to save enough money to put a deposit on their first home and start paying it off. Today's housing investment culture is making it almost impossible for lower income families to even own their own home on the traditional quarter acre block with a yard for children to play in.

The clash of culture can sow the seeds of bitterness and resentment. This can lead to the loss of support and wisdom as different generations distance themselves from each other. Instead of being a source of psychological and financial support, the traditions that proved so valuable in the old world could become toxic especially if the conflict is unresolved and one group interpret the outcome as a victory for one culture or family over another. It is important for younger couples to respect their elders and for both parties to realize the times are changing.

3. The Commercial Culture: the invasion of the entrepreneur

For over 500 years in Western culture the merchants of marriage had been the church and the law. Marriage had been the least entrepreneurial of all human celebrations. The church's role has diminished dramatically over the last 50 years as the number of church weddings declined from 80% to less than 30%. This most recent development has shifted the entire focus from the taking of vows to the paraphernalia of the wedding, the reception, the honeymoon and the recorded video marathon. A new magical thinking seemed to be emerging for those couples who were getting involved in the commercialized wedding industry. This hidden thinking seemed to be that the more expensive the wedding the greater is the couples love for each other and/or the more permanent and happier would be their life together. An added problem associated with commercialism is the advertising which seeks to create new and bigger markets for what is enticing and attractive but not essential.

To live a life of marrying, one needs to ask how relevant it is to associate a level of largely manufactured excitement as the most appropriate and realistic introduction to a life of marrying. Once again, a culture surrounding marriage appears to hinder an in-depth preparation for **the reality of marrying**. More serious is the fact that increased expenditure at the time of the wedding leaves couples, parents or sponsors, facing a huge financial burden paying off wedding debt expenses. This debt can put relationships under extreme stress in the important early days of marrying.

4. The Legal Culture

Originally the legal culture was designed to protect the institution of marriage and property rights. Increasingly it has had to deal with the complicated outcomes of legalized divorce. This is particularly true when children are involved and there are disputes over property. The psychological issues have proved to be extremely elusive to the legal machinery involved. Despite the establishment of special family courts there is increased dissatisfaction with the capacity of the courts to resolve the increasingly and sometimes bitter disputes within families. The legal system has found it particularly difficult to manage the complexities resulting from the Marriage Act of 1975. It has had to adapt to rapidly growing numbers of de facto partnerships in which partners are serious about their commitment to each other and their children.

The legal system has had to adjust to a variety of increasingly complex family structures. This includes blended families, alternating parent families, one parent families, gay and lesbian families, bi-sexual parenting families and transgender parenting families. The *Marriage Act of 1975* was intended to make it more civilized for couples to extricate themselves from a destructive or dying relationship. But, it has made it much more difficult for divorcing parents to parent their children cooperatively. The problem is that freedom always has consequences. The freedom of easier divorce has not prevented costly legal wrangling over access to children, disputes over property and the cost of raising children.

Divorcing parents have experienced greater pain facing the legal costs of disputed parenting than the legal costs of extricating themselves from a loveless and immature relationship. The challenge for those parents, who are no longer partners, is to establish a stable positive parenting culture. As long as our culture continues to trivialize the approach to marrying, easier divorce fails to deliver its promised advantages.

The Relatewell model (2000-2013)

The whole of science is nothing more than a refinement of everyday thinking.
- Albert Einstein -

Evidence is the life blood of research. The Family Relationships Institute has developed an evidence based **anecdotal/narrative** approach to adult education courses for marriage. The goal was to search out what would motivate couples to take an active role in clarifying their personal goals in marrying. This would require designing a process that would enable participants to share their experiences and the individual insights that accompanied them.

The content in the workshops needed to be provided by the participating couples. The educator could involve participants in either of two ways. Ask the couples to list what they believed were the key challenges in marrying, family life, parenting and divorcing. Common insights in their responses were sifted and sorted to identify the common meanings they had for participants. These meanings were presented to a variety of groups of participants. The meanings which received the most enthusiastic responses and proved most able to motivate participants to open up and share their ideas, their experiences and their emotions were the main focus. This material provided the substance for Chapters One to Fourteen in this book.

The second approach was to provide a list of possible areas to explore and engage the couples to choose the course direction. See Figure 1 – Course Voting Process, page 26. The words of Albert Einstein challenged educators to explore whether the process of the Relatewell course was a refinement of everyday thinking and experiences or a requirement tacked on to getting married. The challenge was to make sure the course was an experience which shed light on their day to day living.

As a treating psychologist I was aware that so many mental and emotional problems were a result of a persons reduced capacity to self value and meet the challenge of 'to thine own self be true'.

Another challenge for Relatewell courses was to provide a process that would motivate couples to open up and become active participants. The course had to shed light on issues that mattered to the participants attending.

If there is any implication that participants will need to measure up to some higher standard, then the atmosphere favourable to adults learning would be sabotaged. Participants needed to feel safe from the scrutiny of others. The first and most dramatic task has always been to remove any competitive elements. Participants needed to feel safe in believing that they are not in competition with their partner nor with any other participant. If a person is not locked into comparisons, growth will lead to a discovery of how different we are from everyone else, **not** how better or worse we are in comparison to everyone else.

In 2000, Relatewell adopted an anecdotal/narrative approach to find evidence for what would motivate couples to share openly and involve them in the Institutes' relationship courses. Three hundred couples over a thirteen year period from 2000 to 2013 were involved in shaping a new approach for couples preparing to marry someone who wanted to marry them. Evidence for a new focus emerged. When the emphasis had been primarily on skills, there was always a real possibility of participants comparing themselves with others and fearing to appear inadequate. When the emphasis shifted to the uniqueness of each partner as being the source of their worth, participants began to respond in a lively way and became motivated. Increased sharing and co-operation became more common. This momentum increased when couples were given an open list of areas to identify as relevant to their needs. As the central theme of the course became the importance of being true to oneself, couples became more open and relaxed.

Courses began with a brief introduction on the meaning of **self** and the different contribution of self and **ego** in establishing our identity. Each partner was given a private room in the centre. It was called their **individual space**. Each partner was given a pen, two sheets of lined A4 paper and the questions: 'Who am I'? 'Am I being the person I really want to be in life'? 'What sort of person do I want to be in life'? They were also asked to write down what words they associated with the words marriage, family, single and separated. Once given ownership of the activity, participants began to open up and most filled at least one page. The behaviour of couples in the course began to change significantly. Participants were then reunited back with their partners and given a different room called their **couple place** to share with each other what they had written in their individual space. They were asked to share what ideas they had in common and what were different.

The third activity was to put three couples into small groups, **small supportive communities**. These groups looked for common themes and threads that motivated participants to get involved, open up, share and listen to each other. This experience has taken years to bring to fruition. Up to this point, it had been difficult to get participants to fill in a small activity sheet let alone fill in an A4 sheet with personal material about who I am as well as what sort of person I wanted to become. Now groups did not have to be checked constantly as in previous years to make sure people had not started talking about football, best honeymoon deals, different reception menus and latest wedding attire.

Another contribution of the anecdotal/narrative research approach was that the participants had a major role in deciding the importance of a person's capacity to self value. The couples also needed to be a major contributor to the process and theme of the course. The couples needed to set the core values of the course. The programme was not aimed at fixing participants or nourishing their spirituality. The goal was to promote the psychological growth of each participant. The ultimate goal would be to increase the capacity of couples to marry successfully.

The new approach was confirming that, as in all effective adult education, participants at their courses needed to be self motivating. As long as educators saw their role as one of motivating adults to learn important principles of relating, or that of warning people of the destructiveness of relationship deficits, couples would keep their distance. Both participants and educators would end up exhausted, the educators through their efforts to motivate participants, and the participants through their efforts to avoid exposure. Once the course emphasis shifted to the importance of a strong self as opposed to a big ego, and the ability to self value, couples chose to get involved. Couples' motivation increased further when the emphasis shifted from better relationships to more authentic relationships. The fear of exposure lessened. This new approach kept confirming an important principle underpinning adult education – the primacy of self-motivation. Once the person herself/himself could motivate themselves, the course became self energizing. What did not get couples involved was trying to bump them into the harsh realities of marrying to make them wise before their time.

It is important that in late adolescence and early adulthood men and women were encouraged to enjoy a period of being single without too much responsibility, pressure and stress, but a growing commitment to respect other peoples' rights. This is why it makes sense for young adults to take a year off serious study when they finish secondary school. It is a reason more young adults are marrying later. Thanks to the example of motivated couples, more participants started framing their own significant questions relative to their life situations. The most significant questions for them became 'What sort of person am I really' and 'What sort of person do I want to become as a marrying partner' and 'What sort of person do I want to marry'? These questions have a greater depth than those of earlier generations. People were leaving courses reflecting with sets of new deeper questions such as 'Is this the sort of partner I want to be'?

Questions as a search for meaning – What stood out was the participants' willingness to search for the meaning which lied behind their questionings. 'What does it mean if we can't settle our differences', rather than 'How can we settle them'? 'What does it mean if we can't mend our communication breakdowns', rather than 'How do we improve our communication channels'? 'What will it mean if we don't keep growing up' rather than 'How do we become more mature'? People were leaving courses with a set of new questions and increased confidence that they needed to take themselves and their partner more seriously. People reported a change in their thinking, feeling and choosing in their day to day lives. The new questions created waves of new energy. Couples remained unresponsive to courses which spruik marriage rather than encouraging marrying.

The **anecdotal/narrative** approach has succeeded in ushering couples to work on their experiences of psychological growth rather than their mental and emotional deficits. The evidence that came from Relatewell courses has been expedient. It was important to make clear that the programme was not aimed at fixing the participants but at assisting their growth as partners able to relate well and marry successfully. Until partners saw a meaning to what they were being asked to do, they resisted becoming involved. The meaning behind this approach needed to be based on the centrality of self to achieve a worthwhile life and partnership. The emphasis in the course is not about who I **should** be, but who I really am and the sort of person I want to be. The exercises which made sense to participants and got them involved are recorded in the following chapters.

It is not enough to emphasize that the desire to relate is innate. The problem is that the ability to relate **well** is not innate. It is learned. The evidence was that the ability to be able to share who I am in all my distinctiveness was more important than standing out as better than others, in other words, 'being a good catch'. When a relationship course is structured in such a way that participants can compare themselves as being more or less skilled than others, rather than different in so many ways, people feared exposure. There was evidence that couples responded positively to the view that differences are the ore from which couples can mine the gold in their relationships. The best evidence on which to build a course is the positive responses of the participants. The couples identified a deeper layer of significant variables to assess the effectiveness of a relationship course. These variables are also described in Chapters One to Fourteen and summarized in the Epilogue.

Couples started responding positively to the challenges they were facing in their lives, in particular becoming the person he/she really want to be. If the course failed to help people to self value the course could not succeed. We needed to work with the couples to design exercises that convinced each participant that they had intrinsic self value. See Figure 1 - Course Voting Process. All the evidence pointed to the need for participants to motivate themselves. As long as the educator/facilitator was motivating the course participants, the course was a struggle for everyone involved. As long as the course was focussed on promoting relationship skills or worse, was warning of relationship deficits, couples would keep their reserve. As soon as the course emphasis shifted to the importance of a strong sense of self, couples became involved.

The problem with offering to enhance relationship skills was that participants feared exposure. The ability to relate well is a challenge to everyone. We are happiest when we are learning, except if we believe we are the only one who needs to learn. It is the ability to relate well which is the real challenge for every participant. This ability needs to be recognized as being able to share who I am in all my distinctness rather than standing out as someone better than others. The most serious drawback is not believing I am as good as others. It is believing I am better.

When a course is structured in such a way that participants can compare themselves as being more or less skilled than others rather than different in every way, people will fear exposure. The evidence is that when differences are seen as the ore from which couples mine the gold in their personal and social relationships, couples start to self motivate and the course is energized by the contributions of participants. This book records the evidence on which these claims are based. A striking fact is that couples uncovered a deeper layer of significant variables on which to judge the efficacy of the **Let's Make It Work Courses** and the **Let's Keep It Alive Courses**. It became evident that couples needed to be encouraged to enjoy a time of being single without too much responsibility other than respecting other people's rights and responsibilities. The new level of self-motivation and sharing created waves of new energy.

The one principle that couples responded to consistently was the importance of a strong sense of self which is a theme in this book. The meanings which couples made out of their experiences proved most capable of eliciting a change in their thinking, feeling and choices in their day to day lives.

Anecdotal/narrative descriptions of multiple variables have provided a valuable source of evidence about the participants' responses to life's challenges and the challenges in marrying. It is those who are planning to marry today who can contribute the most relevant material for today's course.

A notable change in today's courses has been people waiting around after a course and not wanting to rush off. The importance of each person's growth sparked confidence not only in a deeper connection with one's partner but with other participants. In the past there was often evidence of particular partners attempting to control their partner's efforts to share with others. Slowly there has been increasing signs of a freedom and confidence, especially in men to take an active role in Relatewell courses. This has been matched with an increasing use of activities and active learning.

INTRODUCTION

There have been fewer participants who have used their verbal skills to dominate their partner or other participants. There was also a reduction in the 'life of the party' participants who in earlier courses tended to dominate activities. This was exciting evidence of increasing involvement by the groups.

It is with this in mind that Relatewell courses are proposed here as suitably expedient for future development of adult models of marital education.

The ability of people to use the quiet moments of the process to voice new thoughts, new feelings and new choices, was exciting. The fifty two years since the original Relatewell course was designed have not been wasted by the Relatewell team. Most impressive of all was experiencing the benefits of people tasting the freedom of being themselves and their attempts to test the limits of their abilities to engage their partner in genuine sharing.

A fresh approach to marrying – a new take on the life of couples

Marrying is an ongoing **process** that brings two willing partners together in a new style of living that involves intimate relating. It has been a constant source of regret to me that the perception of marriage has been oriented to future problems and repeated breakdowns. The theme of this book is an optimistic attempt to remove misconceptions about marrying and to provide new challenging ideas about marrying. It will identify the fourteen qualities, Chapter by Chapter, which partners will need to develop in order to marry successfully.

To create a positive pro marrying culture, it will be necessary to actively involve the whole community in this task. The Relatewell Relationship Building workshops provided grounds for optimism. For 40 years the "**Let's Make It Work**" and

"**Let's Keep It Alive**" workshops have led the way in experiential interactive adult education for relationships. It was no surprise that couples responded to a positive view of relating. They certainly showed little or no interest in identifying or anticipating future problems associated with marrying, except as spectators **not** participants. They do however become involved when their current issues and difficulties are listened to and taken seriously. They become more open to recognizing where their 'now' is heading before it becomes a future that might shatter them.

The workshops provided by the Family Relationships Institute since 1978 provide evidence that a process focused approach is superior to a content focused approach. The former approach enables participants to both validate their experiences and investigate personal qualities required to marry successfully. The word marrying has an immediacy about it. Couples found it easier to open up and share when they realized that they were already experiencing what is involved in marrying. Marrying is not something that lays ahead in the future after you apply for a marriage license. It is today's concerns, today's challenges and today's disappointments that are the relevant material for their growth today to becoming mature partners. The programme constantly reinforced the importance of self and self valuing.

This book also seeks to replace an older pro marriage culture with a new challenging pro marrying culture. At the heart of this culture change will be a primary focus on the personal qualities of the two partners marrying more than on their material achievements and contributions. Any necessary roles in marrying need not be ruled by gender, power differentials or tradition. They will need to be agreed on by the two partners. Each chapter will focus on the principles of equal partnership, mutually agreed on. I am optimistic in the spirit of Martin Seligman's book, *Learned Optimism: How to Change Your Mind and Your Life (1990)*. Two people can marry, achieve intimacy, become loyal stable partners and successfully raise a family.

A fresh approach to marrying emphasizes marrying as a journey and an adventure in which the goal is not the survival of the institution of marriage but rather the thriving of the partners marrying and the children they raise. My thinking is closer to that of a hardnosed reality manual rather than a dreamy eyed visionary brochure.

At the heart of this new culture is the human personal qualities of the two people marrying not outdated rules or roles based on gender, power differentials or tradition. Roles will need to be negotiated continually by partners who see themselves as equals not clones. Relatewell Workshops responded to the participants' need for the immediacy of content. Participants found it easier to open up and share when course facilitators helped them recognize that they were already experiencing in their present relationship much of what was involved in marrying even if they were not yet living together.

Life after divorce

It is the people who have been creatively divorcing who remind us that divorce can contribute a new hope that can help us say divorce is not the greatest tragedy. The failure to learn from divorce is the tragedy. The greatest tragedy is that which children experience when adults don't find a way to compromise.

There is no justification for the attitude "how dare people think they can divorce their first partner and then go ahead and make their second effort more successful than their first".

We need a new culture that can rejoice in the fact that some people can learn to make marrying and building a family a success on their second attempt. Organized religion talks about the need for forgiveness. One way to practice acceptance is by a new emphasis on resilience. Like phoenix rising from the ashes, it is time to welcome those who are repairing the broken relationships from a marriage break up. It is very difficult to mend the feelings of those who have suffered a breakdown in marrying. A good starting point is rebuilding past relationships with a strong new hope of learning to marry successfully the second time around. We need to create a culture free of the righteous attitude that *'you made your bed, now you can lie on it'*.

Just as marrying does not always turn out to be a positive experience, it is important to remind ourselves that there are times when divorce leads to a very positive experience for two people and their children.

Everyone is born with the human capacity to marry successfully

The crisis in marrying is when this capacity is damaged by adult, societal or community villainy and incompetence.

The meaning that two partners give to marrying is influenced by their human qualities not their sexuality. Members of the LGBTQIA community possess the same fourteen human qualities needed by partners to marry successfully. It might be more realistic to debate whether those upholding the institution of heterosexual marriage are more concerned with its identity and legal framework than the wellbeing of those who identify as being LGBTQIA.

As marrying continues to evolve as it has over the annals of time, our understanding of what it means to marry will need to evolve further. The grounds for a modern world view on marriage equality is that marrying does not flourish when it confuses tradition with reality and places the institution of marriage outside the reality of human history. Happiness is not reaching a common destination. It comes from our unique method of travelling which is equally open to both the heterosexual and the LGBTQIA community.

RELATEWELL
Family Relationships Institute Inc

Course Voting Process

Part 1

The biggest challenge you face is to marry, not just get wedded ceremoniously. To marry both partners need a strong identity. There are two paths to our identity: the first is SELF, the second is EGO.

The first part of the course will explore what is meant by SELF and its absolute importance in the challenge of making our marriage and family work. This will compare SELF and EGO.

Making marriage and family work involves a series of challenging transitions. The goal of today's course is to build confidence in yourself and your partner so that you can meet whatever challenges you will face. The greatest challenge in marrying is the fact that as two people commit to their relationship they become more aware of how different they are as individuals. The powerful attraction that brought two people into a committed relationship becomes less pronounced than the gap produced by their differences. We have experienced already this morning the rich diversity of people taking part in today's course. **We now need to design this course to meet your needs.**

Part 2

Participants decide the second part of the course from the list of possible topics offered below. **However, until participants have the opportunity to add to this list they do not have a genuine choice.** Once this is done each participant can **vote for 4 topics** and the order of their preferences is most important. The topics that recieve the most votes become the material for the course.

Figure 1

						The Challenges In Marriage When I Don't Get My Own Way	My Choice and My Order Of Priority		
					1.	Designing a way to marry that works for both of us			
					2.	Managing differences between our family values and culture			
					3.	My responsibilities as an adult partner			
					4.	Managing conflict as a pathway to growth			
					5.	Partners having different needs – What is my responsibility to my partners needs			
					6.	Communication			
					7.	Making good decisions			
					8.	Managing stress			
					9.	How to get closer to my partner			
					10	Managing finance			

Chapter 1
A SHARED MEANING TO MARRYING

Both partners need to enjoy a shared meaning – an understanding of the purpose and what is involved in marrying successfully. The emphasis on meaning will take a different direction to marriage support with its emphasis on specific relationship skills in marriage. At the heart of culture is the meaning it shines on people's experiences, whether they be the chaotic or the mundane. Especially important are those which leave people feeling powerless. Meaning is what helps us to keep alive the best and worst experiences in marrying. These include friendship, companionship, sharing, support, shared sexuality and intimacy. Meaning also helps us reflect on the deeper truths hidden behind the realities that cause our anxieties and our depression. It assists in identifying the significant variables that need to be researched. Meaning is mediated best by those who live out their values in our presence. The writer, Alan Marshall, *I Can Jump Puddles (1955)*, repeatedly quoted his father's advice 'Son, I would rather be sad with the truth than happy with a lie'.

Meaning helps us cope with the passing parade of broken dreams and overcome bitterness. Psychiatrist Oliver Sacks, *Awakenings* (1973), emphasized that it is not enough to be alive. We need to have a purpose for living and a framework for our psychological growth. An awareness of meaning is important because it also offers us a framework for growth through developing purpose and direction. It enables us to manage the worst of broken dreams and finding a way into the best of all lights – hope. Hope is also a guiding light for us in identifying our values and in the ongoing process of sharing them.

Studying the work of psychiatrist Viktor Frankl (1905 – 1997), the author of *Man's Search for Meaning (1964)*, can become a starting point in the search for a shared meaning or understanding of marrying. Frankl spent three years in Auschwitz concentration camp as a prisoner. After World War Two he treated many holocaust survivors. His work led him to conclude that meaninglessness was at the heart of much mental and emotional illness. Frankl himself discovered the importance of meaning during the time he was a prisoner, and later developed a specific therapy for people who came to believe life had no meaning. He called it 'logotherapy'. The scholarly work of Frankl affirms the necessity for all of us to make a meaning to our lives and our relationships.

The primary assumption in Frankl's writing and research is that all human beings have a basic drive to find a meaning to their lives, especially a meaning to events over which we have little or no control. Frankl used case studies to illustrate his forms of treatment. Of one case study he wrote:

> Once, a man consulted me because of his severe depression. He could not overcome the loss of his wife who had died two years before and whom he had loved above all else. Now how could I help him? What should I tell him? I refrained from telling him anything, but instead confronted him with a question. I asked him what it would mean if he had died first, and his wife had to survive him. 'Oh', he said, 'for her this would have been terrible. How she would have suffered! I replied, 'You see, such a suffering has been spared her, and it is you who have spared her this suffering; but now, you have to pay

for it by surviving and mourning her. The man said no word but shook my hand and calmly left the office. He now had a meaning for survival and a way to keep her presence alive.

An ever-present challenge is to make sense of our experiences in marrying and parenting. The search for meaning is critical for us to survive unexpected disasters. In marrying, both partners need to enjoy a shared meaning and understanding of the purpose and requirements to marry successfully. The emphasis on meaning will give new vital direction to the work of marrying. At the heart of culture is the meaning attributed to people's experiences. Especially important are those experiences which leave people feeling powerless.

Prisoners in the wartime concentration camps had very little control over whether they survived or not. The constant theme of Frankl's research and writing is that every experience has potential meaning because meaning is a framework through which each human being can weave their way, whatever experience life delivers. He wrote: 'Whether it was being forced to march or beaten with rifle butts my mind clung to my wife's images. I heard her answering me; saw her smile, her frank and encouraging look. I saw that love is the ultimate and highest goal to which man can aspire.' Frankl realized that it was possible to make sense of what appeared to him to be utterly senseless.

Robert Kegan, *The Evolving Self: problem and process in human development (1982)* and *In Over Our Heads: the mental demands of modern life (1994)*, further develops the pioneering work of Frankl by describing human beings as 'meaning makers'. His work on the four orders of consciousness led him to conclude that making meaning requires the highest order of consciousness. The search for meaning is for Kegan an expression of the life force in both nature and human affairs. The life force in nature rejuvenates forests ravaged by fire and purifies polluted lakes and rivers. The same life force in human affairs can heal deep social ills and crimes by truth and reconciliation. This in turn is a necessary condition for supporting positive and stable families in which children feel loved, safe and valued. By adolescence children need to begin to find the passage to self-valuing. We all need to face the reality that the institution of marriage has an incredible capacity to survive triumphantly no matter how much it damages the hopes of those individuals trying to marry. Kegan's fourth level consciousness enables partners to distinguish the truth and the reality involved in marrying from the repeated promises of the institution of marriage.

A shared meaning to marrying is critical for the two individuals wanting to establish a stable and nurturing family life. It is not enough to criticize past efforts to create a pro marriage culture, we need to bring about a major change in how both the community and future partners challenge their thinking, express their feelings and make their choices.

Understanding the meaning of self enables people to share with each other the sort of partner/person they really want to be rather than listing their achievements or what they bring into that relationship. Meaning is the product of an honest examination of our lives. For Socrates 'an unexamined life was not worth living'. Meaning is the most reliable road to a full life. It helps us to avoid what Albert Einstein described as the greatest human tragedy, the 'many values that die in us while we are still alive'. Meaning gives us something of lasting value to believe in. The biggest threat to marrying is a drought of meaning followed by a deluge of confusion and despair as to what is realistically expected of each partner. Nothing can promote the search for meaning more than the experience of marrying. Meaning is truth growing out of experience, not just theory.

As more partners create positive experiences for themselves in marrying and create positive experiences for each family member, a positive psychological change of climate will occur. A healthy mental and emotional environment for those marrying requires the oxygen of social cohesion and less of the busy competitiveness that underpins an acquisitive society. Each partner needs to find a meaning to their marrying and share their personal meaning. A shared meaning involves constant adjustment on each partner's part. Meaning is made and sustained by the values established within families and community. Marrying involves an affirmation of fundamental values which are the pathway to meaning. The power of meaning in turn draws attention to values as an expression of the life force described by Frankl and quoted in his letters.

The enduring values underpinning a meaningful pro marrying culture

Value 1: Life opens up in the real world - avoid fantasy

> The quality of the relationship is one of the most important factors to move from an emphasis on surviving in marriage to thriving through marrying.

Value 2: Balancing differences is more enduring than surfing attraction

> Marrying requires a life of loving, resilience, sharing and supporting on the part of both partners to produce the gold of companionship, loyalty and intimacy.

Value 3: Life is not always fair or just

> Life, which includes nature, people and society, is not always fair or just. Nature gives us fair warning of this, yet nature itself is generous and lavish; beautiful parks and gardens, a sunset, seaside and moun-

tain view are nature's gifts. Yet nature can also be unstable and treacherous: tsunamis, earthquakes, fires, disease and pestilence are part of our relationship with nature. Likewise the object of our attraction can give way to an emptiness, an unreliability, a spitefulness or a disillusionment. Attraction carries no guarantee of permanence. A firmer basis for partner selection than simply attraction is required.

Value 4: A strong self is the firmest basis for fidelity

To marry successfully both partners need to keep building a strong identity.

Value 5: The need to keep growing up

Partners need to achieve, maintain and grow to a level of maturity that enables them to negotiate the demanding transitions in adult life which occur in marrying and raising a family. We need a culture that convinces us that we need to keep growing up.

Value 6: Adults need to know their responsibilities

The essence of being adult is a capacity to know what our responsibilities are to our partner and family. Even more critical is knowing what we are not responsible for.

Value 7: Marrying is a lifelong process

Partners need to know that learning to marry and raising a family is a lifelong process of experiential adult education. Each partner needs to become a mentor to the other.

Value 8: Criticism and contempt are an abuse of power

Power, control, criticism and contempt are the most effective way to nullify partners' efforts to marry successfully.

Value 9: Short term luxuries are single life experiences

Every personal journey and adventure needs those involved to make personal sacrifices. Marrying requires that both partners are willing to give up some freedoms and space. These are short term luxuries confined to those living a single life.

Value 10: The need to be real people not perfect people

To enjoy marrying requires the same effort and experience it takes to enjoy living. We don't have to be perfect, rather, it certainly helps to be real.

The search for meaning is not a rapid exercise, it requires intimate sharing of their thoughts, feelings, choices and values by each partner. It is meaning which helps us to reflect on the deeper truths which are hidden behind the facts that cause our anxiety. Statistical analysis can deepen our concern and expose the variables that need to be identified. The meaning of this information, however, is beyond the reach of statistical analysis. Our personal health is bound up with our answers to these questions:

1. What does it mean that people who begin marrying in an atmosphere of hope and joy too often end up bored, confused or embittered?

2. What does it mean that so many children are psychologically damaged by caring parents who become warring parents?

3. What does it mean that too many children end up being forced to take sides in adult conflicts?

4. What does it mean that family violence is increasing in the home, and that for too many women the home is the most dangerous place to live?

5. What does it mean that too many parents have been unaware that their children have been sexually abused by relatives or trusted friends within the home?
6. What does it mean that there can be so much pain in raising a family and so much psychological harm done to children by parents who love them?
7. What does it mean that, despite this mayhem, marrying remains the universal choice of behaviour across all nations, cultures and epochs?

The biggest challenge most people face in life is to find a meaning to living, marrying and parenting. These three human behaviours involve periods of confusion, helplessness and pain as well as joy and contentment. Without meaning we are left to wander blindfolded through a series of painful experiences which leave us mystified. This extends Frankl's conclusion that meaninglessness is at the heart of existential neurosis. This illness develops with our failure to find a meaning to the constant flow of disappointments, let downs and crises as well as life's most rewarding events.

The search for meaning is critical for those seeking to marry successfully. We cannot find, let alone make meaning, through statistical measurements. A worthwhile life begins with the inner journey to the self. If we put this journey on hold at any stage of life, a sense of isolation and meaninglessness can slowly engulf us, therefore it is critical that each couple agree on a shared meaning to their life of marrying. As a philosopher, play writer, novelist and political activist, Jean-Paul Sartre repeatedly said: 'Everything has been figured out, except how to live.

Chapter 2
A STRONG 'SELF' IS ESSENTIAL

To marry successfully, each partner needs a strong self-identity. The four concepts or pillars central to establishing one's own identity are:

Pillar 1:

Each partner is a person who has inalienable rights both in society and in the context of marrying. This is the path to freedom both in society and in the family.

Pillar 2:

Each partner is an individual. Each person is special because they are essentially different from everyone else. This is the path to diversity and multi-culturalism.

Pillar 3:

Each partner has an ego which establishes their position in society on the basis of their achievements. For a few, this is the path to success and acclaim. For too many, it is their path to insignificance.

Pillar 4:

The self: the core of a person. The self is who I really am as well as who I really want to be. The self is defined by its human qualities and less by its achievements. It is the path to intimacy in marrying and belonging in community. See Figure 2 – 4 Pillars Of Identity, page 46.

Psychologists treating mental illness all too frequently witness the fact that betrayal or suppression of one's true self is a major source of guilt, depression, frustration, shame and anger. Such negative emotional states make it difficult to marry successfully.

The three most powerful and popular ways to develop a strong sense of self are to marry, to parent and to play an active role in building up community and society. Marrying is something partners do, it is not something done to them. It is time to put an end to what I consider to be farcical language that we 'got married'. We can 'get robbed' and we can 'get trapped' but we cannot 'get married' – rather, we 'marry'.

What do we mean by 'self'?

The self is the core of each person's being. It is the essential truth of who a person is. The self is not who a person is told they should be or who the person wants to be. Deep down a strong self resents being told who they should be. The basis for my own self acceptance is the same basis for my acceptance of everyone else. What we as individuals have in common is that we are all different. From birth it is clear that even identical twins are profoundly different. The Chinese philosopher Lao-Tsze wrote that 'He who knows others is learned. He who knows himself is wise'. Gilbert K Chesterton, writer, wrote that 'Everyone on earth has something to give to the world which cannot otherwise be given. That is their self'. The self is dynamic and needs to keep growing.

Figure 2

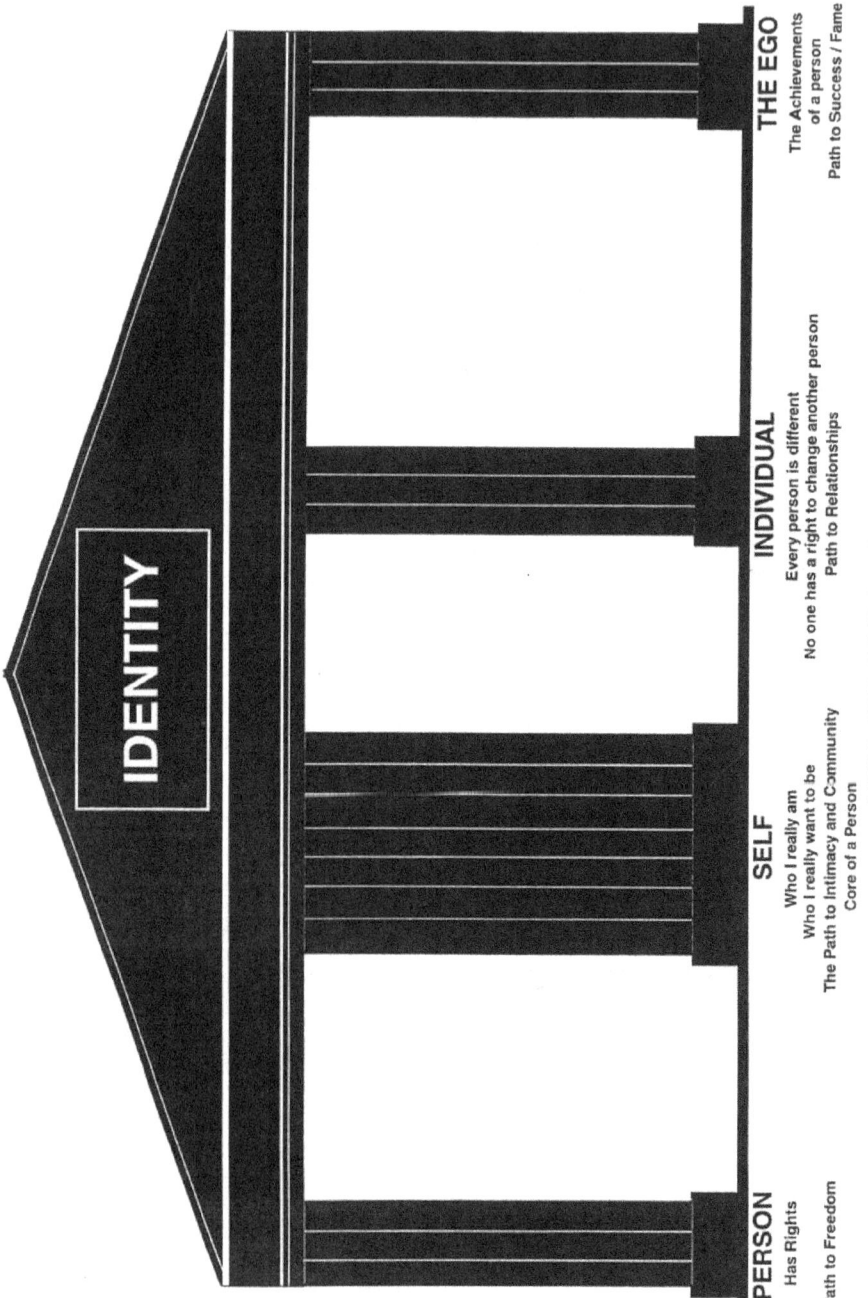

The self is greater than the sum of all of its parts so there is always more to learn and discover. The self may experience doubt because it needs to keep growing and learning in order to have a meaning for living. The self takes responsibility for its actions: it does not blame others. The self has an unquenchable desire to share itself. The self will not give peace to those who ignore it. Saint Augustine wrote: 'Most people go forth to wonder at the height of mountains, the huge waves of the sea, the broad flow of the ocean, the course of the stars – and forget to wonder at themselves.' To really know a person, we need to know something of the self of that person.

Marrying requires two strong selves not two large egos. A strong self can help us deal with life's most difficult choice 'Who will I choose to make my partner, my companion and my friend for the journey and adventure of marrying'? Some wise insights into the individual self belong to the first century Gnostic* texts discovered in Egypt in 1945: 'If you bring forth what is within you, what you bring forth will save you. If you do not bring forth what is within you, what you do not bring forth will destroy you'.[1] This text indicates a depth of understanding of the meaning of the self as the essential truth of a person.

Understanding the self is important for those who wish to marry successfully. We can think in the following terms: If I fail to express my true self I risk ignoring my true self and settling for living in the shadow of the egos of other people. While not everyone has a large ego, everyone needs to have a strong sense of self.

We need to explore the meaning of the word 'self' to appreciate its importance for people to be able to marry. Everyone

---

* The Gnostic Gospels are 52 texts discovered in Egypt in 1945. The original texts are dated between AD 350-400. They are a collection of Christian Gospels and writings including the Gospel of Thomas and the Gospel of Philip. As the early Catholic Church became more institutionalized, many Christian writings were not included in the New Testament. Much of the rejected sayings were called heretical.

has within them a strong core that we call the self, which will not be denied. Marrying has meaning when both partners gradually reveal to each other the deeper and more significant part of who they are – their true self.

Marrying thrives within the union of two strong selves. The self is dynamic, searches for the opportunity to grow and constantly seeks to express itself. It is a lot more than a person's reputation and individuality. The self is a mixture of light and dark. The challenge for all of us is to ensure that the light in us dispels our darkness rather than the darkness in us extinguishing our light. There is only one of any person and their kind and thoughtful acts live on in the memory of their family and friends once that person dies. When we focus on our self, or another self, there is always more to learn and discover. I believe that the philosophy of the self is that life is to be lived not squandered.

The meaning to marrying is that it is a journey of discovery and adventure with some difficult transitions. The pace of change keeps intensifying in adult life. The self has an unquenchable desire to share itself. When marrying, both partners need to challenge each other.

One important question the self will demand to know is: 'do I prefer to be a grown-up or a person who is growing up through life's challenges?' If we stop growing, we risk behaving as hollow partners and parents. The tragedy is no one is born this way: we are born to experience curiosity, challenge, intimacy, insight and to make a change in our world. A worthwhile life begins and ends with the inner journey to find our true self. The English essayist, poet, and antiquarian Charles Lamb (1775-1834), while on his death bed is reputed to have said to a friend: 'Who I am now is who I have always been.' Lamb believed he found and knew his true self.

A STRONG 'SELF' IS ESSENTIAL

The vitality of the self can be seen soon after birth

The vitality of the true self can be observed in the newborn child. The healthy baby bursts onto the scene and explodes into life. Every cry and action is a clear statement of their self valuing. They demand to have their needs met. They demand to be taken seriously with cries that mean 'Here I am, feed me', 'I am soiled, clean me', 'I am awake, nurse me', 'I am tired, rock me', 'I am awake, where were you?', 'I can crawl', 'I can walk' and more. There is no doubt on the part of the baby of its own importance, no guilt, no apology. The first primitive expressions of the self can be a shock. Positive parenting is a challenge.

What needs to be mirrored back to the growing child and the emerging self is affirmation and praise. Life begins with the promise of greater things to come. The only parenting failure at this stage is an adults' ignorance of the child's true nature. The most important early source of self valuing is the feeling of being loved as a child. This process needs to be supported throughout life. It includes making friends at school, enjoying learning as an adolescent, establishing close relationships as a young adult and finding meaning and purpose as a mature adult.

Leading an authentic life

A significant risk in early childhood is when parents are unaware of the need of the child to create an authentic sense of self. The focus needs to be on the full flowering of the new self, and less on the defeat of the dark forces that can invade it. The self is not in competition with other selves but seeks partnership and connection. Self valuing comes from a quiet confidence that 'I am a worthwhile and decent person'. See Figure 3 –The Self Tree, page 52.

The following case study illustrates the depth of meaning of the word 'self' and its crucial role in enabling both partners to lead an authentic life as well as the ability to each share their self in marrying. I once treated a woman who was a highly successful surgeon, but her passion was painting. Although everyone respected her knowledge, skills and dedication, no one admired or loved her. Her family had arrived in Australia in the 1960s. Her great-grandfather was an eminent surgeon, as was her grandfather and her father. The woman was the oldest of three girls, and as there was no son she was expected to carry on the family tradition in medicine. She was the most brilliant of the siblings and had topped her school. She loved her father and did what he expected of her. She had the ability to easily complete her medical studies and complete her training as a specialist. She was eminently successful in her discipline.

Despite success and fame in her career, there was a profound frustration and anger within the core of her being. She had a divided self. Her true self was suppressed. The phoney self was the eminent surgeon whom everyone respected, but no one could get close to. Eventually the woman gave up medicine and went to art school then art classes.

Through art she had found a peace and happiness which she could not find as a nationally recognized surgeon. She has found peace and happiness without needing to be acclaimed as a leading artist. It was not fame and success but an ability to express her world in art that enlivened her existence. Respecting her true self, she found what mattered to her – she found direction and purpose in her life. When I last saw her, she was happily marrying and happily sharing the parenting of her twelve year old son.

We do not need to become an eminent or successful person to have a strong self: we are born with a strong sense of self. We need to make sure that we do not allow anyone to damage our core sense of self or belittle the kind of person we really want to be. There is a Russian saying: 'Keep your hands off my soul'.

If I fail to express my true self, I run the risk of not developing a sense of self. An even worse outcome would be to settle for living in the shadow of other people's egos.

Enlightened selfishness is evidenced in people who are able to enjoy or find satisfaction in whatever they do, whether it is helping other people, pursuing some creative past time on a hobby or simply having fun. Unenlightened selfishness is characterized by a life ruled by excessive duty and unremitting responsibility with overtones of resentment and a 'poor me' attitude.

The destiny of the self is reflected in the plasticity of the human brain. The newest portion of the brain, the neo cortex, enables us to develop concepts of self. What enables the self to evolve is the process of differentiation. The cells in our body are made from the same material. It is through a process of differentiation that our cells evolve unique properties which in turn enable us to perform separate yet related functions. The greater the differentiation, the more sophisticated and adaptive is our life form. The self is the powerhouse of differentiation. To understand the importance of having a strong sense of self, we need to understand the difference between self and ego. Everyone needs a strong sense of self and it is up to each person to grow it. Not everyone has a big ego. The cost of having winners is that there have to be losers.

Figure 3

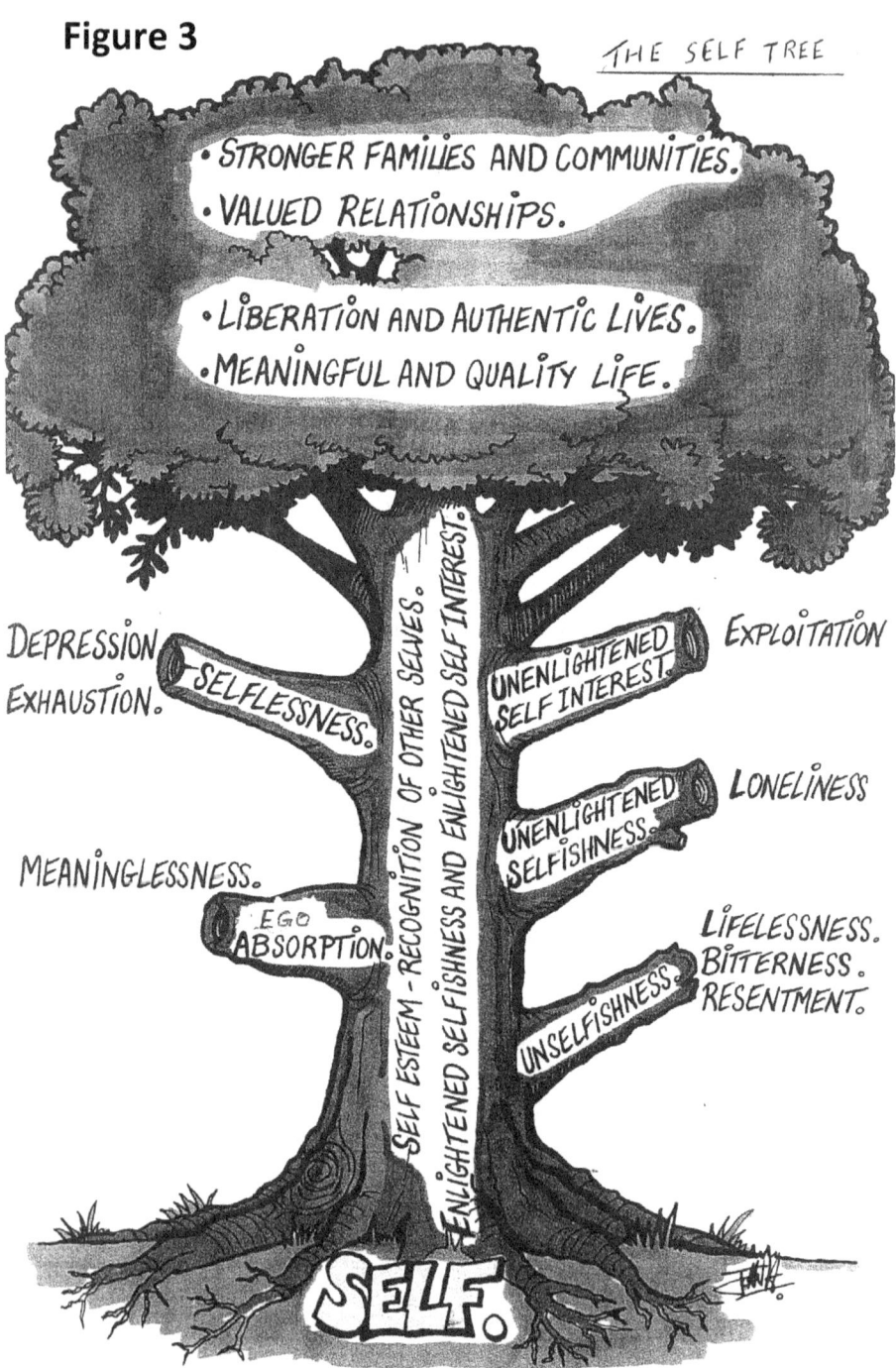

Chapter 3

INCREASING OUR SELF VALUING QUOTIENT (SVQ)

The next challenge for partners seeking to marry successfully is to learn to raise their self valuing quotient (SVQ). This, in turn, leads to a more fundamental question: What do we mean by self valuing? How do we get it? Is it like the Australia Day Awards given only to a deserving few? If we believe that self value is simply two words **self** and **value** bestowed on a privileged few, we will struggle to understand the depth of its meaning and its importance to every human being.

The term 'Self valuing' has many synonyms. 'Self esteem' sounds a little highbrow while 'Self love' can have a narcissistic implication. 'Self acceptance' has a hint of duty, 'Self regard' and 'Self respect' can introduce a power differential. 'Self value' therefore emerges as the most challenging and appropriate.

It is clear that before marrying, we all need to establish a strong sense of self. The next challenge for partners seeking to marry successfully is to learn to raise their self valuing quotient (SVQ) – the 'quotient' being a unit of measurement. The most common experience of those professionally treating clients with marital or psychological problems is not just the difficulty of an accurate diagnosis of their problems, it is treating the clients' low self valuing quotient.

The meaning we give to self will be critical in determining the meaning we give to life and especially to marrying. Partners wanting to marry successfully need to understand this and to keep raising their self valuing quotient. Self valuing is more than a phrase made up of two words. It is a sentence with a subject 'I', a verb 'give', an object 'my self' and a predicate, 'value'. The complete sentence then becomes, 'I give myself value', or to express it another way: 'self valuing'. Only I can give my self value. To become famous I need other people's acclaim. To feel successful I need to be noticed by others. For example, if their football team wins, fans want to touch their heroes and supporters line the boundary to slap hands. Successful people, more than most other people, need to be able to give themselves value. It is not surprising that too many famous young people commit suicide or suffer from alcohol or substance abuse because they do not feel valued. It is important to balance fame and success with a core sense of self and self value.

The two founding fathers of Psychiatry, Sigmund Freud and Carl Jung, fell into a bitter dispute over their different interpretations of self and ego. It is not surprising that there is confusion within the discipline of Psychology over the meaning and definition of self and ego. Self and Ego are constantly used interchangeably despite the fact they are totally different.

The question which best illustrates this is: 'Who do you think you are'? Depending on the questioner's tone of voice, this question can provide two diametrically opposed responses. If the tone of voice is encouraging and reassuring, the question is an encouragement to share 'who I really am'. It is an opportunity for an affirmation of self. However, if the tone of voice is sarcastic, disparaging or disapproving, the question can become a total put-down of the person being asked. The problem is more complex when considering the concept of self. If the self is who we really are, and an entry point to sharing our qualities and our identity, why do we tell children to be **un**selfish or worse, not to be selfish? It is best to tell them to be caring of others.

Problems can arise with the language used when people are trying to raise their quotient or measurement of their own self value. We need to expose the contradictions when we associate with the concept of self with concepts which are totally opposed to the meaning of self. For example:

Self Absorbed: The combination of self with absorbed is a nonsense. The healthy self seeks growth and intimate connection with others. This is hardly consistent with being absorbed. It is when we allow ourselves to be absorbed by money, greed, power and fame that we run the risk of failing to treasure the most valuable qualities in our self. It is not a problem to be absorbed in the growth of our self or other selves. The cause of much unhappiness in marrying and much psychological pain is when we fail to take seriously the growth of our self and substitute a phoney self for our real self. A strong self is focused on growth but not absorbed by it.

Self Abuse: The combination of self with the concept of abuse is a further nonsense. How many lives have been ruined by unfairly associating the concept of life long growth of the whole person as being invalidated by an extremely narrow focus on self pleasuring? Self-abuse can mean self-harm.

Self Sufficient: What a sad state it would be to never experience both the joy and the frailty of unrequited love. Hiding under sufficiency is a disowned self, fearful of being hurt emotionally. The price paid is the loss of joy through connection with others and the wounding of the self. The self needs to find meaning in both sufficiency and insufficiency.

Self Control: The self does not need to control life. It accepts that life is not always fair and just. The concern of the self is to take a serious interest in its world. The self's interest is its power to express itself more fully to share 'who I really am'.

When discussing the self, the above phrases are best be avoided. The concept that does sit most comfortably with the word 'self' is the word 'aware'. This combination expresses the self's search to be more alive and looking for opportunities to keep growing. In contrast to ego, the self is not keenly competitive. It would rather involve others in its journey of discovery than leave others behind. Awareness includes time to relax and smell the roses. Locking up the concept of self in a cell with inappropriate company, the self will never cease trying to escape. Some avenues of escape are disastrous – money, power, exploitative sex, alcohol, drugs and fame. These are the failed substitutes for an active questioning mind. This leads us to the real challenge for every person.

Childhood and adolescence – learning to be a partner

The first step has been to clarify the importance of a clear understanding of what is meant by self. The second step is to isolate those experiences in childhood and adolescence that are critical to meeting the challenge of adult life which is to keep growing up and raising one's self valuing quotient or score. The first school children attend is their own family. There are three experiences a supportive family needs to provide each child.

Let me begin with a case study. An indigenous young Australian woman was being interviewed on television. She was vivacious, articulate, happy and creative. She spoke about her wonderful family life and her outstanding mother. She mentioned that her mother loved her as an only child. She described her relationship with her mother as the basis for the wonderful life she now enjoyed with her six siblings. 'Hang on a moment, you said you were an only child' the interviewer interrupted. 'That's right', the young woman replied.' 'But now you say you were an only child.' The young woman responded: 'Our mother told each of us that she regarded all of us as special, and in that sense she loved each one of us as an only child.' Each one was loved but loved differently.' Listening to the young woman speak, it was clear she had a liberating and strong sense of self, a mature ability to share her thoughts, feelings and choices. She was a very real illustration of a person who was able to keep increasing her self valuing quotient. Her charm had depth. The fact is that it is much easier to increase our self valuing quotient if we had, during our childhood and family life, been convinced that we were special because we were different.

Adolescence is much more difficult to negotiate. What had bonded girls and boys in primary school was the culture of accepting everyone because they shared something in common. They were all different in their own way. In adolescence the script for membership of the group changed dramatically. Being of value because I am different gave way to schools promoting excellence. Students were being valued because they were better than others. It seemed very easy to seduce children into accepting this new culture. Adolescents find themselves being valued because they give value to their school.

Self valuing is becoming dramatically different. It requires adopting a more competitive lifestyle. The way to self value shifts dramatically from an authentic way of being a child to someone who is increasingly corralled into being better than their peers in as many areas of school life as is possible. The school, the media and peer groups subvert the truth that each individual is unique and special in their own way.

This is the crisis of adolescence. The message often becomes 'you are special because now you are better than others' or 'You are special if you are welcomed into the in-group'. 'You are special if you are more attractive, if you can perform better in class or on the sports field'. Life becomes a jungle of competitiveness. The adolescent's world is turned upside down. You become an object of envy if you are successful. There is little joy in each other's success. The most powerful expression of worth is to be a winner. No longer is it because I am different. The pressure is to give glory to their school by being outstanding in sport and in studies. The pressure is to be successful not necessarily authentic.

Like generations before them, lack of authenticity is the major source of alienation and anger for today's youth. The novel by J D Salinger, *The Catcher in the Rye* written in 1951 is still regarded as one of the best English language novels of its era. It was the first novel to tackle the issues of adolescent angst, innocence, identity, belonging and loss. For the novel's anti-hero, Holden Caulfield, the world had lost its meaning, everyone was fake, and they did not believe in anything. Holden Caulfield could not find a connection with his peers. He raged against the fakeness of his world and the fakeness of people wearing an identity that lacked authenticity.

Young people need to have agency in their self-definition and to have a say in forging their future. Adults need to be aware why youths spiral into self-hatred and explode into acts of violence against themselves. David Bowie warned that 'these youthful victims spit on us as they try to change their world.' An important role for parents is to recognize destructive, negative thinking and cancel it out. We must encourage youths and adolescents to raise their self valuing quotient by channeling their vital energy into a positive expression of their true self and if necessary moving from a sense of victimhood through survival and on to thriving.

If competitiveness becomes a life style it will eventually spill over into every area of life including marrying. Students even compete to have more likes on their smart phones to indicate how many friends they have. The self needs to be the organizer of our thoughts, emotions and choices rather than the media or our peer group.

Chapter 4
VALUING THE DIFFERENCES BETWEEN PARTNERS

When it comes to mining the gold in marrying, it can be very difficult. Yet, without realizing it, a considerable number of couples treat marrying as though they believe there is a good chance that they will keep stumbling on large nuggets of 'relationship gold'.

Marrying involves two people building a unique connection as they keep discovering how different they are.

If partners 'fall for each other', they can easily overlook their differences. This may succeed, but often only for a short time. Experiencing and accepting their differences is the process of successful marrying in action.

The longer two people live together as committed partners, the more aware they become of their differences. This is in addition to their common interests, beliefs, values, mutual attraction and active sexual life.

Often people began therapy complaining: 'This is not the person I married' or 'I just want to get back the partner I once enjoyed' or 'My partner has changed beyond recognition'. 'It is as though our marrying was just an affair and it seems all over now.' The reality is that when most people choose to marry, they are certainly choosing to have more than an affair.

Often they have not prepared themselves to recognize and adjust to their differences.

Recognizing and adjusting to differences

When two people choose to start living together as marrying partners they begin moving from a connection based on shared chemistry, interests, values, tasks and goals into an ongoing process of discovering their differences. This leads to a long process of adjusting to how profoundly different each other really is. Often people begin therapy complaining, 'This is not the person I married' or 'It is as though our marrying was just an affair and it seems all over now.'

What is valuable in therapy or courses is the evidence that participants are keen to share their ideas and the increased level of their personal sharing. When given the opportunity to contribute to the process of a course or a treatment session, a transformation occurs in the participants. Comparing the outcomes when participants see a meaning to their experiences and its relevance to their present life with the negativity of the earlier responses of participants is enlightening. Insight on this brings a significant shift in partners' mutual involvement.

Nothing causes the initial attraction of partners to fade more than the fear of rejection based on an erroneous belief that deep down 'I am not good enough'. Our society is full of people whose sense of self worth has been seriously hurt, sometimes criminally lost because they are different. Underneath this mentality is an erroneous belief that my partner needs to be the same as me because that validates me.

Family therapist Terrence Real speaks of what is a powerful experience for many marrying couples: "There comes a moment when you roll over in bed and think it's all a mistake. That is the first day of your real marriage." It is a familiar conclusion, but one that has sometimes led to successful partnerships.

The former Prime Minister Gough Whitlam and his wife Margaret are among those better remembered despite being immersed in politics and public life for over 60 years. They married successfully and raised a family. They experienced sacrifice, pain and joy in their individual lives. They became closer in their own relationship. Theirs was an inspiring example that successfully marrying is realistic and attainable by people in busy public lives.

In summary, once partners feel free to be themselves in marrying they are close to the next important task. That is, for each to become the right sort of person to each other. To become the right partner will require some adjustments, some shared pain, and the rewarding realization that their partner has become the exclusive right one. Simultaneous with that realization is another important insight. There are many more persons out there that they could have married successfully.

A word of caution

What are sometimes described as differences maybe more pernicious than two different intellectual viewpoints. It may shelter a disdain for the person with the different viewpoint. Bridging differences requires a genuine respect for each other on the part of both protagonists. The goal is not victory and triumph, it is a growing understanding and respect for each other.

Chapter 5
BEING A BRIDGE BUILDER

What is meant by a model for marrying? A model is defined as providing a simplified description of a system, or situation devised to facilitate an outcome. In an issue so highly personalized as marrying, a model needs to value the profound difference between the two partners marrying and their interpretation of what is the best process for marrying. It should alert a couple to the challenges that may be ahead and encourage personal growth. These are the keys to marrying successfully.

The model needs to be simple and have potential applications for many. The couple themselves need to give voice to what they believe is the best applications of the model. The model which makes sense for partners is the model which allows for maximum diversity. The model's strength needs to be its relevance to the life of marrying. A suitable model needs to elicit non-threatening positive responses from each marrying partner at different times.

A model for marrying cannot promote universal marketable solutions nor idealized programs. At best, it can help different people to come up with effective personal strategies. There is no area of life more private than marrying, and this is the reason individuals and couples are usually resistant to what they may determine is an invasion of their privacy. For too long people running relationship courses wrongly concluded that couples were resisting change and growth. It was more a fear of appearing immature or protecting their privacy.

In the early days of relationship education many courses used couples as models. These couples were selected because they were regarded as excellent models for young inexperienced couples. They were happily married and their family life was strong and supportive.

When I trained as a volunteer educator in the 1960s I remember attending one particular session on pregnancy. The session leader was a warm attractive woman in her early forties with a good sense of humour. The small group of trainees observed the young couples listening, spellbound by the presenter. At one stage she was talking about the challenges of bringing up her two teenagers. While the audience were entranced by her presentation style, her experience made no real connection to this group of future parents. It became clear that the 28 participants were seduced into enjoying the story teller's experiences in parenting. This example stands out in my memory because it did not seem to matter to the attendees that the course they were attending was advertised as a relationship building program for couples planning to marry.

The lessons learned from the training experience were significant. An effective model was needed to help the participants explore their own experiences and gain insights they could immediately put to use. None of the participants had children of their own and only two couples were pregnant. The people running the course were passionate believers in marriage and family life. They were blissfully unaware that the model for each couple wanting to marry successfully cannot be another couple's model. Not only is each partner different, so is each couple. No couple can model marrying or parenting for another couple.

A model for couples marrying needs to address the fundamental challenge in marrying successfully. The Simon & Garfunkel song *Bridge Over Troubled Waters* focused on the wrong target, 'troubled waters'. This emphasis took workshops back to an earlier failed model. Couples have shown little interest in what could go wrong. This model has been constantly rejected in favour of a more applicable model, making marrying and raising a family an issue of thriving rather than surviving. The real challenge is the growing gap between partners who had been so strongly attracted to each other but were becoming increasingly aware of their differences. The most worrying issue for couples marrying is the presence of a widening gap as differences become more significant.

What would enable couples to bridge this gap? The content of the courses needed to focus on new powerful emotions of disappointment, loneliness, neglect and confusion as couples experience growing apart. The solution is for couples to acknowledge and understand the meaning of their unique gap. The cost for neglecting to bridge these differences is their potential to explode couples apart. The solution is for couples to develop strategies to meet half way across their identified area of difference and discover its potential to unite couples more closely than ever. The bridge needs to be strong enough to support the increasing traffic of marrying. This includes a deeper sharing of thoughts and feelings and the many daily and repetitive tasks of family life.

In the more practical issues in life, there is no hesitation to model behaviours in business, sport or fashion, all of which are highly competitive areas. Models for achieving our personal goals, like marrying, are far more difficult to design. Such models need to be idiosyncratic not imitative. No person can be a better model for marrying than the individual who is trying to marry. The best models in marrying need to leave room for each partner to imprint their unique self on the finished product. Couples are willing to share themselves if both partners are prepared to listen.

The Sydney Harbour Bridge

By the late 1920s the city of Sydney faced an enormous challenge. A huge gap existed between Sydney on the South side of the harbour and the suburbs on the North shore. Hundreds of ferries were needed to take commuters back and forward. If there was fog, people would be faced with very long journeys. The Labour State Government decided to build a bridge and chose a single arch bridge. Sydney Harbour Bridge is the world largest, but not the longest, steel arch bridge in the world. Construction commenced in 1923 and the bridge opened in March 1932. Sixteen men lost their lives building the bridge.

A single arch bridge is built in stages, as is marrying. The first stage is securing the foundations. This was helped by the fact that Sydney is built on solid rock. The second stage is building two spans each beginning on opposite sides of the harbour. The third stage is pushing the two spans across the gap to meet and form a single arch. The final challenge is to ensure that the two spans meet perfectly. Two facts are critical: each span must be self-supporting until they lock in perfectly together. The fourth stage begins in the very middle of the arch as the sections of roadway are dropped down from the arch. The fifth and final stage is when the roadway suspended from the arch is completed and the traffic flows freely in both directions across the bridge. Herein lies an effective analogy and insight into an apt model for a couple attempting to marry. The greater the weight of the traffic on the roadway, the stronger is the connection of the two spans, and therefore of the bridge.

A metaphor for bridge building between couples

The Relatewell approach involved groups of couples who were in search of an effective model for marrying. The outright winner was the Sydney Harbour Bridge. Like all bridges, the

Sydney Harbour Bridge exists to facilitate the traffic of people and goods across a great gap. Marrying involves the constant traffic of each partner's thoughts, feelings and choices to achieve intimacy. It is important to understand the resistance of couples to marriage preparation courses. Let some of the partner's speak for themselves when expected to do a pre marriage course:

- We already know each other really well.
- We know all about each other so there is nothing more to learn.
- I've been married before so there is not much that I don't already know about marriage.
- We fell in love at first sight. That's enough for the moment.
- We knew from the beginning that we were just right for each other.
- Both our families agreed we are an ideal match.
- We share a similar culture so we already understand each other.

I once asked close friends whether they would encourage their twenty-five year old son and their twenty-three year old future daughter-in law to attend a pre marrying relationship course. Their answer was very defensive, 'I think we've done a pretty good job with our kids. Why would they need a course?' The framework for supporting partners must address the concerns and questions of the current generation, not the concerns and questions of previous generations who often were more concerned with the institution of marriage than the people marrying.

In Relatewell courses, it was interesting to compare changed motivations after discussing the Sydney Harbour Bridge model. Participants showed a dramatic change in their involvement. Slowly but surely participants began sharing their insights.

The question to address was 'How can a bridge made of steel help people think creatively about marrying?' Slowly but surely participants began contributing. Some of the couples' contributions, recorded at the time, speak for themselves:

> For us to stay unconnected for long periods could break up our commitment.
>
> It is the fact we keep connecting that is more important than getting married with a piece of paper.
>
> It made me question whether our commitment is strong enough to lead to an ongoing connection.
>
> Marrying requires its own arch. It can't be steel. We need to search together.
>
> The arch is the strongest structure in engineering. The greater the weight of traffic on the bridge, the stronger the bridge. We can use problems and the tough times in marrying to make our loving stronger.
>
> The bridge was built for two way traffic. The two way traffic in marriage is both partners sharing thoughts and feelings and supporting each other in home making.
>
> Just as they adjust the directions of traffic flow in morning and evening peak periods, so we need to adjust our lives out of concern for each other.
>
> I have rarely thought about our differences being as important as what we have in common.
>
> My partner had an opposite response. I questioned whether we were sufficiently connected. He had no doubt.
>
> What gives meaning to marrying is the link between connecting and committing.
>
> What impressed me was each couple has to build their bridge their way and where they want to build it.

The two spans had to be self-supporting until they make a strong connection. As adults we need to be able to stand on our own feet and not lean too much on each other.

Every single working day the steel bridge is being scraped of rust and painted. Marrying involves constant maintenance and upkeep.

It made me think more seriously about the balance between connection and commitment.

The bridge has proven to be an effective model because of the numerous parallels between building a single arch bridge and building a marrying relationship.

Two-way traffic for both bridge-flow and marrying presents a similar challenge

The greatest challenge in supporting partners to marry successfully is handing over to them the power to control both the process and the direction of educational experiences designed to make marrying and parenting work for each member of the family. This will involve a shift in culture from preventing or reducing divorce to promoting the need for partners to commit themselves to their personal growth and the growth of every member of the family. Put simply, the term 'grown up' needs to be replaced by the term 'growing up'.

What I mean by a model is any process which can contribute an insight or meaning to an important area of life. What was discovered at Relatewell workshops was that if people are given ownership of the process of adult learning they become self motivating, open to thinking positively and expressing emotions less self-consciously. They are more likely to choose to share with others. The journey of marrying requires constant adjustment by couples to the growing gap between them. The most successful model is for each partner to be a bridge builder.

Bridge – Figure 4, Span

Restraining cables are clearly visible in this view from Bennelong Point as the fourth panel nears completion, August 1929

Bridge – Figure 5, Unconnected Spans

May 1930

BEING A BRIDGE BUILDER

Bridge – Figure 6, Connected Spans

1930

Bridge – Figure 7, Deck Assembly Progress

Deck assembly progresses with creeper cranes backing down arch,
December 1930

Bridge – Figure 8, Sydney Harbour Bridge Completed

Chapter 6

THINKING, FEELING AND CHOOSING

There are three fundamental psychological measures of a decent human being. These are the ability to think, to feel and to choose. Partners wanting to marry successfully need to practice all three. It is also necessary to recognize how distinctly different these human capacities are played out. This is not as easy as it looks and can be what brings many people into psychological treatment. They are experiencing being stuck. Common presenting problems are expressed as: 'Nothing much happens between us any more', 'My partner has changed' or 'I want him/her back'. Until the conversation shifts to genuine feelings, the couple are stuck in an internal debate that swamps emotional pain but doesn't drown it. We need to practice thinking, feeling and choosing, both in our work and our relationships. This is how we come to learn that we need to value the three measures in different ways.

- We value thoughts by challenging them
- We value feelings by sharing them as personal gifts rather than as grenades with the pin pulled.
- We value actions by judging their outcomes fearlessly and with integrity. It is important to judge actions rather than the person who commits the action.

Feelings are never right or wrong. The thinking that is associated with them can be adaptive or maladaptive. The actions that result from feelings can be productive or destructive and therefore right or wrong. Our thinking and/or our actions can certainly divide families, communities and nations. We need to discover the potential for shared feelings to unite people. This is true for positive and negative feelings. Thinking contributes to informed choice, the source of our dignity.

In Oliver Stone's 1989 film *Born on the 4th of July*, a crippled soldier has accidentally killed his nineteen-year old lifelong friend and neighbour when they were ambushed by the Viet Cong. The survivor's life had descended into a life of alcohol, drugs abuse and self-loathing. He eventually finds the courage to face the family of the dead soldier. When the mother answers the door, he is choked with pain and says: 'I'm the one who killed your son'. The mother replies 'We understand what you have been going through. We have both suffered'. They embrace each other. The pain of loss eased as they opened up their pain to each other.

To understand the power of feelings that can heal, we need to recognize that they are pools of psychological energy. We need to find a constructive way to put this energy to work. All feelings are real and need to be shared. Sometimes it is the pain of our inner spirit that seeks release. At other times it is our body that seeks relief. To fail to share our pain risks an explosion of pent up emotions.

Some radical principles for managing feelings

Every feeling is OK. The only way to divide feelings, is into positive or negative. A positive feeling is one which any mentally sound person wants to hold onto, for example, happiness. No healthy person would say 'I'm sick of feeling happy'. A negative feeling is one which any person in their right mind would not want to continue feeling, for example, shame or despair. No reasonable person would say 'Help me feel more terrified in a real world situation'. Here are some thoughts on dealing with our feelings:

All feelings are real: we need to share our feelings and value the feelings that people share with us.

All feelings are a form of mental and emotional energy. Depression can weigh us down like gravity. Anger can send blood rushing to the face or drain it away. As with physical energy, there is positive and negative mental and emotional energy. We are learning that in our world all energy is limited. We are learning slowly not to waste any form of energy.

We cannot control our feelings: we can manage them. We can learn to postpone the gratification of allowing our anger to explode through lack of discipline. We can't afford to allow particular feelings to spin out of control.

We need to own our feelings. We need to assess our level of responsibility for how we feel rather than blame someone else. That is what children do. Rather than accusing someone else of making us angry, taking responsibility for what I choose to do.

We need to identify our feelings. We need to know when we are sharing a feeling and when we are sharing a thought. There is nothing more capable of confusing communication than a thought dressed up as a feeling. The give-away is the insertion of the word 'that' in the following sentence. 'I feel **that** you don't love me as much as you used to'. There is no such feeling as 'you don't love me as much as you used to'. The person uses the word feel but it is followed with a belief not a feeling. In effective communication, a feeling needs to follow the verb 'feel'.

The next question needs to be: 'How do you feel if you believe your partner doesn't love you as much as they used to'? In this situation the person is more likely to share how they feel, e.g. they feel sad. This in turn is more likely to open up communication rather than continue arguing defensively about how much they feel loved or who is the better lover. There is a simple rule to facilitate communicating feelings. All feelings can be used constructively or destructively. Positive feelings can be used negatively, for example: I feel happy when I am at the beach so I won't turn up for work this week. They can be used positively, for example: I am going to work hard each day so that I will have enough money to spend my holiday at the beach. Negative feelings can also be used constructively, for example: I am angry with my partner for always ignoring me at parties so we need to talk this issue through. Or, I can use negative feelings destructively, such as: 'I'll punish him by going to bed early to avoid sex'.

We need to find a constructive way to share our feelings. The best way to do this is by sharing them as intimate gifts of oneself rather than by dumping them on others where they can become poisoned darts or hurtful missiles.

We need to find a constructive way to respond to other people's feelings. The best way to do this is not by trying to solve the problems which cause them emotional or mental pain but by listening empathically to their story. The new radical method of turning communication into a positive experience will be explored in Chapter Ten.

Integrating thinking, feeling and choosing

The further challenge in developing our three fundamental capacities to be decent human beings is to balance and integrate these three capacities. How this can be accomplished is exemplified in the following case study.

I once treated a man who worked three jobs. No toy was good enough for his children. He wanted his two sons to have the best. He never forgot his own childhood which was characterized by poverty and arguments over money. He swore his sons would never go without. He was a man of action. What he didn't realize was there was no emotional connection through sharing of feelings and spending time just enjoying each other's company. Everyone was expected to be happy. When this didn't happen, the father struggled with a belief that he was a failure.

Feelings were totally pushed aside. They were too painful to talk about and think about. Attempts to control feelings and remove any sadness were his priority. When he was home the mother had to keep the children quiet so that the father could get the minimum five hours rest/sleep. At Christmas time there were a variety of expensive toys all beautifully gift wrapped. The children, however, spent most of the day playing with the balloons, the colourful wrapping paper and playing taxies in the large cardboard boxes.

Some years ago the father suffered a stroke. He could no longer work long hours and buy expensive gifts. Slowly overcoming the effects of his stroke and difficulty in walking and talking, he could now play with his sons and the family could laugh and cry together. This father had overdone the action dimension of human kindness but neglected the need to think his way to a more balanced involvement with his children.

His early relationship with his children had a single dimension. It was love by action. He was buying love through expensive toys. The saddest feature was what the man wanted most from his children was for them to love him. The 'little boy' within this man was desperately repeating the losses that marked his own childhood. His own father was rarely home and the son felt neglected right through his childhood. Now he spent his life trying to buy his sons what he had always wanted but never had experienced. The father had become disillusioned when his two sons showed little interest in the expensive toys he bought them. Now he too was spending his life trying to buy his sons the love he never had.

The big breakthrough in this man's life happened when he started to feel his frustration and sadness, believing his sons did not value what he himself had always wanted as a small child and had worked so hard to give them. In therapy he eventually shared the sadness of his own childhood and the anger that he felt when his sacrifice seemed to mean little to his two sons. He was helped through treatment to open up his grief and loss and share it. He experienced the relief of letting go past sadness and the shame of believing he was an inadequate father. He also came to realize that he was a generous father whom his sons wanted to love, play with and have fun while enjoying positive feelings of warmth and security.

If someone chooses to present arguments that are one sided and biased, they lose credibility. This is particularly true within a family. We value thoughts by ensuring that both points of view are equally presented and documented. In marrying, it is critical that both partners are given equal time to express their point of view. Thoughts can be correct or incorrect, true or false. A stable, positive family life also requires rigorous thinkers who have learned to challenge their own and each other's thinking. We have come a long way from the days when children should be seen but not heard. We need to encourage children to think for themselves and speak up. We all need to listen and challenge our own thoughts and those of others. We need parents who model these values. This ability to challenge negativity may be achieved by couples – and their families.

In summary, our thoughts, feelings and our actions need to be balanced and integrated. Consider the following:

- How I feel can determine how I behave and how I think;

- How I behave can influence how I think;
- How I behave and how I think can determine how I feel. A life spent on obsessive reflection lacks balance as does a life focused exclusively on feelings alone. A life spent in compulsive judgement of my actions, or other people's actions, can lead to judging people, rather than their actions, and eventually to the paralysis of social initiative and a lack of shared values.

The need to distinguish thoughts, feelings and actions is paramount because we need to value each of the big three measures of our humanity differently. Our choices, our thoughts and our feelings will influence our understanding of the importance of the power differential in marrying for good or ill.

There are two types of power. There is personal power which enables a person to flourish by becoming the person they want to be. This power helps partners develop self skills. These include thinking freely, feeling deeply, enjoying simply, caring lovingly, acting justly and living courageously.

The other form of power is institutional power which involves power over others. Prizing power to control others, can become a pathway to domination and resentment. History reminds us that all power over others can corrupt us and absolute power can corrupt absolutely. To choose power over others often involves investing time and money in cliques, treaties, liaisons, subjugation to authority and loss of identity. Sadly, too many marriages have become institutions in which members have struggled to survive.

When partners and family members develop their capacities to function at a higher level of awareness, the way power is distributed between partners will affect how they feel about each other, what they really think about each other and how safe and stable is their commitment?

Chapter 7
A MATURE ADULT IS ALWAYS GROWING UP

What does it mean to be an adult? Legally it means that I have turned eighteen years of age. Psychologically it raises a very big question. Can we afford to stop growing up? Is becoming an adult one of the miraculous transformations of modern life? A child at seventeen years and eleven months becomes an adult at eighteen. The challenge in living a full life is that each life stage needs to be an experience of continual constructive learning. We need to learn how to live as children, then how to live as adolescents and finally how to live as adults.

The French approach to ageing is not to ask: 'How old are you' but to ask 'How many years do you have?' The French approach is a reminder that every year of adult life is an opportunity to learn something new and achieve something of value. The biggest challenge in life is to realize that growing up needs to be a long term process of personal growth. We cannot remain forever youthful, but we can recognize that the biggest challenge in life is to discover that growing up is a long term process of personal growth. We need to focus on perpetually 'growing up' rather than being 'grown ups'.

Adult life needs to be a search for new sources of vitality. The meaning of vitality changes as we keep growing up. There is not much value in presenting physically as a thirty-year old if my ability to think, feel and make choices are more redolent of a seventeen year old. It is not unreasonable to re-define an adult as someone who is seriously committed to keep on growing up.

It is worth reflecting on the length of the three main periods of life. Adulthood is the longest transition in a person's life. Childhood is approximately twelve years from birth to age twelve. Adolescence is approximately six years, twelve to eighteen. The average life expectancy at birth for women is eighty-four years and for men eighty years (ABS Statistics, 2016).

Another perspective on adulthood is to define it as a transition from the freedom of being single with its increasing lack of accountability to the sober realities of adult responsibility. What can poison the long journey of adulthood is the belief that I had 'grown up' by the time I turned eighteen? Another problem is the folksy belief that people will wake up to reality once they 'get married'. We do not have to function as an adult to 'get married'. But, we do need to function as a maturing adult to 'marry successfully'.

Marrying requires two adults who are both growing up rather than two adults indulging themselves with the thought they are already grown up. Five issues stand out for adults wanting to marry successfully:

1. there is the commitment by both partners to keep on growing up;
2. a well developed sense of responsibility;
3. an understanding of the role of dependence, independence and interdependence in marrying;
4. the centrality of interdependence in marrying successfully;
5. the need to use personal power to become more responsive to each family member and connect more deeply with them.

Except in adolescence, all growth is a slow and gradual process. It is measured by the quality of the person's physical, mental, emotional and spiritual growth. Marrying involves managing a lifelong process of maturing. A mature baby does not automatically become a mature child and then a mature adolescent and finally a mature adult. Families need to promote growth and qualities more than achievements.

The centrality of interdependence

Maturity is the journey from dependence through independence to interdependence. The essence of dependence is expecting someone else to meet my needs. Dependence revolves around what the other person can do for me. The risk is that dependence may encourage a less secure person to seek help from more and more people.

Dependent people need others to give them what they want. Their attitude is:

> I need you to take care of me;
> you will support me;
> you look as though you are kind and loving and will look after me;
> you won't let me down;
> you are to blame if I am unhappy or have had bad luck.

Independence revolves around me and my efforts to meet my needs:

> I can feel;
> I can think;
> I can choose;
> I am responsible;
> I am self-reliant.

Independent people usually get what they want through their own effort. If independence allows a person to roam free and this quality is not balanced by some commitment to another, it can lead to a very lonely life.

The essence of inter-dependence is that I remain responsible

A MATURE ADULT IS ALWAYS GROWING UP

for meeting my own needs but I choose to do this sometimes by winning the support of a significant other. Inter-dependence revolves around **us**:

we can get more of what we want by working as a team;
we can make a life together through mutual support and sharing of thoughts and feelings;
we can pool our talents to create something bigger than the two of us;
we are better able to meet whatever challenges life places in our paths.
Interdependent people can combine their own efforts with the efforts of others to achieve a more meaningful life.

Children respond most of all to parents who enjoy life, their partnership and each family member. These parents make very good models by example. Families need adults who are learning to integrate and balance dependence, independence and inter-dependence. There are times when one family member will need to be dependent on another such as when someone is ill. There are times when one or several members of a family will need to be independent of other family members. This could be in their choice of career, their choice of a partner or the way they spend their money. More dependence can sometimes put pressure on a partner who is responsive and generous. Too much independence can lead to someone using the family and the family home as a convenience but failing to contribute to the general running of the home. The reason that inter-dependence needs to be a core component of marrying successfully is because it requires partners to keep listening to each other before making decisions, to keep supporting each other and to keep sharing their innermost thoughts and feelings. This enables them to respond genuinely to each other.

It is critical to understand that inter-dependence is not simply a combination of dependence and independence. It is a totally different concept, introducing a totally different perspective. It also establishes a different connection with reality.

Mature adults know what they are responsible for, what they are not responsible for and to whom they are responsible. Taking responsibility for making the other adult happy and sexually fulfilled can deprive an adult partner of the opportunity of developing important insights into the nature of adult responsibility. Each person's responsibility is to be a partner in growth rather than a rescuer or a fixer. At a deep level, mature adults can end up feeling resentful for being rescued. The goal is to help partners to discover their fundamental responsibility in marrying which is to support each other by sharing. Experiencing support can help people discriminate between my partner doing something for me to rescue me, as opposed to someone encouraging me to try doing it for myself and eventually succeeding. Central to the challenge of discovering the secret of inter-dependence is open positive communication that enables partners to reveal themselves in greater depth to each other.

Much anxiety in marrying is due to an insecurity that can magnify a person's need to please others at the cost of diminishing a deeper understanding of the complex responsibilities in marrying. The most complex responsibility is inter-dependence. Mature relationships are characterized by a realistic assessment of adult responsibility. The most mature level of responsibility is an inter-dependent one.

Friendship between partners is sabotaged when the meaning of responsibility is unclear. True responsibilities can be ignored and fake responsibilities exaggerated. Freedom is a half-truth when it is divorced from the most important qualities of an adult – responsibility. A functional adult needs a balance of wisdom, common sense and sometimes cunning to survive risks to their conscious and pre-conscious thinking. A responsible attitude is a saving grace.

Marrying is too important to find any reason to absolve ourselves from creating a vigorous and realistic pro marrying culture. At the same time there is no basis for believing that marrying is the best choice for every one or that some people should be excluded.

Co-dependence is effective at producing family martyrs but not mature partners.

Co-dependence is a destructive force in marriage. It occurs when one partner set out to prove their worth by rescuing the other partner who has a problem eg: gambling, alcoholism, affairs or a deep rooted psychological disorder. At the same time the person with the problem is becoming co-dependent on their interaction with the fixer. The added difficulty is that the motivation for these patterns of interaction can be unconscious.

Being an adult involves putting our mind, heart and soul, including our smallest acts, into growing together rather than winning.

Chapter 8
TAKING OUR OWN NEEDS AND OUR PARTNERS NEEDS SERIOUSLY

Maslow's Hierarchy of Needs

Abraham Maslow's *Hierarchy of Needs* provides a theoretical basis for shifting the priority in marrying from surviving to thriving. The goal of thriving was my rallying cry when I was the Director of the Family Relationships Institute. Education for marrying was slowly redefined as a process to help people set and reach their own personal goals for marrying.

The ongoing act of marrying involves five levels of needs:
- The first level is the need for survival, food and shelter.
- The second level is the need for security/safety.
- The third level is love and the need to belong (community).
- The fourth level is a need for what is variously called self-esteem, self-worth or what I call self valuing.
- The fifth level is the need to self-actualize.

Marrying is presented as a shared journey by two people who support each other's efforts to meet their developing needs. The layers in the triangle illustrate that as partners mature mentally and emotionally, their needs deepen. The *Hierarchy of Needs* used at the Family Relationships Institute became a major agent of change in the work of the Institute.

An important goal for people preparing to marry was to see marrying as a series of open doors inviting them to new possibilities of growth and development and a fresh meaning to marrying. The emphasis would no longer be on marrying as a revolving door of vows made, neglected, broken, renewed or sometimes finally ruptured. The new focus would be on the importance of each partner taking responsibility to meet their deepest needs and supporting their partner's efforts to do likewise. Often the challenge in marrying is that partners are at different levels in the hierarchy of needs. This is one of the gaps that partners experience in marrying and requires partners to be 'bridge builders'. A major role in marrying is to encourage each other's development when one of them is struggling.

By 1978 at the Family Relationships Institute regarded helping marriage to survive was no longer seen as a sufficient goal. The preliminary emphasis in marrying shifted beyond the issue of domestic roles and relationship skills, important as they are, to discovering and meeting individuals and partners' needs.

This emphasis took pride of place as an essential process in marrying and in the growth of each and every family member.

The needs model is a complicated process that requires thinking freely, feeling deeply and choosing wisely. There are two important principles underlying the hierarchy of needs model.

The first is the necessity for each partner to meet the first basic level of survival. Only then is the person able to begin the move to a higher level of need. The basis on which a worthwhile life is built is survival. When survival is threatened nothing else matters. To fail at the first level of need is to risk a life of poverty with little or no motivation to move on.

The second principle is that each new level of need, as it is met, evokes the next level of need. The five layers helped to emphasize that each need grows out of the fulfilment of an earlier need. As a more basic need is met, the next level of need becomes more consciously desired.

The triangle is an important feature of the model. The triangle standing on its base emphasizes that the basic needs are the first priority and foundation for higher needs. Maturity becomes the ability to recognize what is my present authentic level of need. It is immature to think that I can leapfrog from an early second level of need to a fifth level of need, or any other intermediary level of need, because it seems appealing. There are no short cuts on the road to maturity. Each level of need must be experienced to reach the ultimate goal of the fifth level of need, self-actualization. Maturity is the ability to recognize priorities. The triangle is most stable and difficult to topple over when it stands on its true base.

Summarizing the five Levels of Need

The first level of need in the journey of marrying is for partners to meet their need for survival through food and shelter. When this first level of need is met, people experience the force of the second level of need which is security and safety. It is not enough to enjoy food and shelter today if the person doesn't know whether they will have food and shelter tomorrow or in the days following. When a person believes they have a safe and secure future, they are fulfilling their level two need for security. A level three need for belonging will now be aroused. This third need is met through being accepted in community. Acceptance is given to those who become active and constructive in family, friendships and community. Once this third level of need is met, a fourth level of need becomes more pronounced. This is the need a person has to not only self value but to experience being valued by others. Once this fourth level of need is experienced, a fifth level of need is triggered. This is the need for self-actualization. Experiencing the fifth level of need is consolidated when a person's self-valuing is affirmed by their peers.

No one wants to believe that death will mean they will disappear without trace. People self-actualize in many different ways. The most common way to do this is to raise a child to be a decent respectful human being. Other ways could include playing a significant role in building a more civilized human society, philanthropy, being an activist, a distinguished public servant or leaving a legacy of positive relationships. Some people self-actualize by reliving golden memories and reflecting with satisfaction that they have expressed the person they really are. It is important to understand that a person does not need to marry to self-actualize. However, the qualities that enable a person to self-actualize are a critical component of marrying successfully.

Marrying is evolving – today more than ever

This issue is much more than an intellectual debate. It goes right to the heart of what it means to be a human being. Here we can address the fundamental questions: are full human rights bound up with a person's genitalia or the focus of their sexual attraction? Is every child who is brought up by a single parent or a divorced parent disadvantaged? There is no psychological or sociological data to support the view that the 'normal' nuclear family always produces well-adjusted children who become well-adjusted citizens. There is historical evidence that many wonderful people have been brought up by responsible adults of the same gender. There is evidence that the divorce of parents has a profound effect on their children. Child psychologists agree that most children rarely give up hope that their parents will get back together. Their sadness is at time acted out by destructive behaviour against themselves, their parents and/or their siblings.

A brief history of people marrying

At the heart of the fierce determination of recent opponents to equal marriage rights is an ignorance of the constant evolution of marrying. This has occurred over centuries from the time humans first formed into tribes and gradually settled into societies with their own laws and culture. As previously mentioned, Sociologist David Dawkins argued that marriage has always been an evolving reality. Family and marriage appeared about the same times in human history as agriculture. Before farming, people lived in hunter/gatherer communities.

There is evidence that wedlock has been an evolving phenomenon since the earliest days of the human race. The earliest societies were built around a promiscuous matriarchal culture. Part of the evolution of what we know as marrying has been due to the transition in society from foraging to farming. The evolution of marriage has been rapid and dramatic whenever there is a significant cultural or economic shift in civilizations. Today we are witnessing a profound change in courting rituals such as online dating due to the information technology revolution.

Chapter 9
INTEGRATING LOVE AND ATTRACTION

The ability to translate emotions of affection, attraction, admiration and desire into the actions of sharing, supporting and enjoying is called 'Action love'. By contrast, 'Romantic love' is being swept along by passion and a desire to maintain a couple's current intensities. Both love and attraction are powerful life forces that can lead to incredible joy and unbearable pain. The confusion centered around these two powerful forces is compounded by the contradictory language we associate with them. No word has suffered such deranged interpretations and twisted meanings as the word 'love' and the phrase 'to fall in love'. Sometimes male clients state that they 'love their kids to bits'. Then you hear the mother, who is now a sole parent, has been left to pick up the pieces. Clients often say that they 'fell in love' with each other at first sight. Others say they want back the person they fell in love with.

There are very few things of great value that we can fall into. Greek mythology emphasized that life is like a river and it is impossible to step back into the same river twice. We can fall into a river and if we can't swim, we could drown. We need to remind ourselves that every thing in life, like the river, is in a state of flux. The life we step into as a young twenty-year old can never be repeated. It is the nature of the river to keep flowing. It is the nature of things to keep changing.

Life requires human courage. A farmer may be close to

growing a record crop only to witness it washed away by a 'once in a hundred years torrential downpour'. We can't just hold onto the powerful positive experiences of life or its fantasies. We need to prepare ourselves for the next challenges. We can experience a powerful attraction to another person, but we can't freeze that moment in time and make it permanent because life, like the river, flows on. Even if we could fall in love, we can't stay in love: it is not a permanent state. We can make the most of this powerful experience we label 'attraction' to show our best side but we cannot freeze these experiences in time, re-name it 'love' and make it permanent. The one most permanent experience in life is action love.

We need to understand the difference between powerful attraction and building a powerful bond of commitment to an ever-changing object of our desire who, 'like myself', has a right to grow and change. Talking about the permanence of love is a very tricky subject. Our love or lack of love changes everything. We can't fall into a permanent state of love because we can't keep loving the same person in the same way. This would be the path to boredom. We can only love as the person we are today, not the person we were ten years ago. What is more, we can only love our partner, as they are today, not as the person they once were.

People ask whether there is anything permanent in life. The answer is a resounding 'yes'. It is what I call action love. Who wants to fall into making the most important decision in life? Stability needs to guide our choice of a future partner and the co-parent of our children. Attraction plays a powerful but brief part in our life choices. How many people have learnt to regret their choices to rush into marrying? The old sating is 'Marry in haste and repent at leisure'. Attraction can express that a powerful new hope and vitality is coming into our lives. It is action love that will heal, revitalize and make our deepest hopes take flesh.

Sadly, we don't prepare ourselves for what often happens in life such as the occasional dashing of our hopes. We need to remember that attraction is basically a phenomenon of nature over which we have little control. The challenge in loving is that we need to keep distinguishing the difference between love as a human experience and attraction as a life force of nature. The challenge in human loving is to integrate the two very different dimensions of love and attraction. Our relationship with nature is much more complex than our relationship with another person. It is disappointing that our decision making in terms of marrying sometimes seems more like a lottery than a thoughtful questioning. Very few people win the lottery. The problem is the nature of language, especially when love is confused with attraction.

The biggest challenge is to integrate the different contributions of love and attraction. The first experience is being swept off one's feet. This can involve the joy of mutual attraction, or the agony of a negative response, or worse, an absence of any response leading to confusion and self-doubt. There is no greater joy than reciprocal attraction in the early stages of a relationship. It builds up confidence in our personal worth and the humanity in our judgements. This escalates rapidly in the context when nature's lavish generosity surrounds us with good health, beautiful places in which to relax and to discover the many dimensions of relating happily. Attraction is a natural experience and is not to be disrespected but understood and recognized.

There is another side to nature. It cannot always be trusted. It can be treacherous and unreliable. Nature expresses itself in raging bush fires, tsunamis, earthquakes, famine and disease. The same principle applies to nature's gift of attraction and our desire to connect passionately and permanently. This is why we need to rehabilitate the expression 'to fall in love' and expose its shallowness, its temporary vitality and tragic risks. Nature, primarily, is concerned with perpetuating the human species. It is not concerned with the wellbeing of the individual person wanting to connect meaningfully, passionately and loyally with an object of desire. Any force of nature can be creative at one moment and destructive at the next. An earthquake can shatter a mountain or a city. We cannot take our enjoyment of anything in nature for granted. In matters of 'love', human beings can fall for each other. Nature sounds a warning when it makes sure that it is painful to 'fall out of love'. We cannot take our enjoyment of anything in nature for granted.

There is another life force in our nature that is reliable and ready to intervene. This is the force which brings the community closer together to respond to natural disasters. It is the force that brings immediate help to victims of tragedies. The food parcels, the donations of money to rebuild, the tradies donating freely their time and skills and the million acts of kindness by people who don't even know the victims are evidence of this force which I call action love. **Action Love** is a verb and a doing word, an action. The continuing contributions over years to help restore hope, life, homes and infrastructure does not fall out of the sky. They are the result of countless actions of support, both big and small, by fellow humans. This force helps communities recuperate. In the long run this force is more stable and powerful than the destructiveness of nature, but it takes time and effort. This force, called 'action love', or 'grace', is called on repeatedly by victims of nature's destructive forces. Every couple and family member determined to succeed in marrying needs to recognize that family is the most stable source of action love.

'Falling in love' is the nearest that some prosperous white men and women get to a cargo cult mentality. The mistake is to believe that future intimacy will be measured by the intensity of the initial attraction. The beauty in the natural world carries no guarantee that it will last forever. We cannot take our enjoyment of anything in nature for granted. As adults we need to nourish the force of action love within us. Above all as parents we need to make sure that this force is not extinguished or sullied in our children on their journey to adulthood.

If we interpret the ebb and flow of our impulsive attractions as an experience of 'love', we will expose ourselves to a belief that love is also fickle. If we believe we can 'fall in love', it is not surprising that we can come to believe we can fall out of love. It can lead us to absolve ourselves from the responsibility to take seriously the most important choice we will ever make in life: the choice of a partner with whom we will explore the meaning of love, pain and 'the whole damned thing'.

Recalling the response of the whole community to the destructive force of nature, in Victoria's Kinglake and Marysville bush fire disasters in 2009, we become aware of a more powerful force that resides within us all. It is a sleeping giant ever ready to be aroused and to intervene. This is the force of **Action love** which resides in every one of us and within our community. It is such a powerful but gentle force when aroused. It unites the broader community to respond to the natural disasters by bringing immediate help to victims of nature's tragedies. The million acts of kindness demonstrated by people within the community are not things that we 'fall into'. They are action choices, the best expressions of 'action love'. Action love is our guarantee that our society will not sink into chaos and barbarism. Action love is not something that we can confine to our family or our neighbourhood, it is spread by example. It is spread by doing.

Chapter 10

COMMUNICATING AT A DEEPLY PERSONAL LEVEL

Effective communication is an essential tool to enrich the interpersonal relationship between partners. Very few of the communication courses that couples attended prior to attending the Relatewell communication module were capable of enriching interpersonal relationships between committed partners. Interpersonal communication skills are designed to provide a process to facilitate opening up and sharing between partners. The major resource utilized is the experience of both partners. The focus on communication within the family and especially between adult partners was the process in which both partners experienced a new level of sharing. A communication course needs to be shaped by the experiences of the individual participants, the couples and the community which the couples create at the course. There is no manual to ensure success. There are experiences which, if managed sensitively, will ensure each partners growth.

It was a frequent experience at Relatewell courses for some participants to announce that they had previously completed communication courses both at school and at work. It became clear that the context in which those Communication courses that were being offered needed to be carefully examined and set apart. The context of staff development and work based training communication covered a vast range of loosely related work skills. They included updating technical skills in IT, handling difficult clients, improving staff ability to successfully conclude sales and creating loyalty to the corporation or firm through team spirit. In the school context communication also covered a vast range of topics. They included stamping out bullying, sex education, road courtesy, safe driving, successful job seeking skills and eradicating behaviours which could give a school a bad reputation. All of these so called Communication courses had very little cross-over impact on improving interpersonal communication and the possibility of increased intimacy.

Communicating for partners who want to marry successfully is a most highly developed skill both in terms of content and in terms of process. How we need to communicate when marrying is far different from any other context. For a start, the stakes in marrying are of the highest order. They include each partner's sense of identity, their capacity to be intimate, sharing their uniqueness, revealing their vulnerability and sharing their lives at a deep level. More importantly it includes choosing a partner with whom to have children and learning to parent them sensitively.

Communication for people marrying is like a diamond. There are many different facets of communication depending on the context or the intention. If my intention is to relate socially with my partner, I need to communicate at a social level. I need to develop an ability to describe events in my life, report experiences and tell jokes.

If my intention is to influence my partner, I need to learn different communication skills – persuading, convincing, motivating and planning.

I need to learn to respond to my partner's efforts to do the same. If my intention is to relate cooperatively with my partner and look for answers together, I need different communication skills such as brainstorming, hypothesizing and explaining. If my intention is to relate intimately with my partner by becoming more open, caring and revealing, I need to develop another set of communication skills such as sharing thoughts and feelings. I need to disclose who I am by making 'I' statements, listening and giving feedback. Modern marriage requires communication at a variety of levels but especially at the intimate level. Communication at an intimate level requires a reciprocal flow of thoughts and feelings between two people.

The following case study illustrates the importance of clearly defining communication. The couple had come to see me for marriage counselling. When asked to describe the problem they wished to solve together, the woman replied 'our lack of communication'. The husband turned to me and said:

> I have no problem with communication. I run a business. Every one of my workers knows exactly what they are to do and how they are to do it. In fact, I am also an Officer in the Citizens Military Force. Every one of my soldiers knows what their orders are and how they are to discharge them. So you can see that I have no problem communicating. It is my wife who has the problem. I have no difficulty telling people what I want, and they have no difficulty in understanding my instructions.

In the context of marrying, this man was a poor communicator. His wife on the other hand was an effective communicator. She was able to express how she felt. She had felt lonely, hurt and disappointed for several years. She was also able to express her thoughts. She believed that her husband had no respect for her because he did not try to understand her need for interpersonal communication and failed to give her emotional support. It became clear that the husband was not willing to listen, let alone change.

It took the wife two sessions to confirm her belief she would destroy herself if she stayed in the marriage. She was ready to act and she chose to leave the marriage. Consistent with her choice to leave her partner was the calm expression on her face and her relaxed body posture. What she felt was more than relief; it was acceptance that she had done her part over many years to really connect but without success. For too long she had felt depressed and blamed herself for the lack of communication.

The three channels of communication

Communication for people marrying involves a reciprocal flow of personal thoughts, feelings and small choices which add up to a serious commitment. The first and most important channel is **action love.** To maintain a flow of support and sharing three channels are needed. Very few will dispute the timeless saying that actions speak louder than words. Many of us, at some stage in life, may give only a notional assent rather than a real assent to this saying. If we fail to recognize any of the three channels of communication we place ourselves at risk of being poor communicators and therefore partly crippled lovers.

The second channel of communication is **words**. A popular singing group, the Bee Gees, sang 'Its only words and words are all I have to take your heart away.' If we exaggerate the importance of words but fail to recognize either of the other two channels, our communication will end up off balance.

The third channel of communication is **body language**. John D Loudermilk reminds us that body language is as powerful as the song and the lyrics in *The Language of Love*. The song *Plaisir D'Amour* is another reminder of the power of the body language channel and its volatility, 'Your eyes kissed mine and I saw the love in them shine'. Marrying has meaning as a journey in which partners seek to reverse the reality expressed in the words, 'the joys of love are but a moment long but the pain of love can endure the whole night long.' The challenge is to integrate each of the three channels action love, words and body language, as essential components of effective communication.

A gentle touch is far more powerful than a persistent mauling. A passionate kiss has greater potential than a gentle absent-minded peck on the cheek or a routine kiss when leaving for work. The message in each channel needs to be consistent with the message in the other two channels. If we say we love someone we can't afford to keep resting our eyes on a stunning looking woman at another table. If a partner writes a love sonnet as well as Shakespeare but dedicates it to someone other than their marrying partner, they are sending an inconsistent message and undermining the nature of both loving and communication. If you can't keep a permanent job because you prefer regular dream time or relaxing with marijuana, you lack credibility as a supportive partner. You are a partner with a divided loyalty. Your action channel is badly blocked.

Communication needs to be a sharing of our complexity and the light within us. A reveal all confession is not always a mature behaviour, especially if it involves a dumping of my guilt on my partner.

A key factor in committed relationships can be the power differential between men and women. The lack of value placed on women's work is reflected in lower rates of pay. Pregnancy can leave women seriously disadvantaged in the workforce. It is even more difficult for the person who has willingly sacrificed career and work experience for home management and child rearing to fight for legal rights against an ex-partner who is so much more cashed up. In particular, it is reflected in reduced welfare payments to single mothers who often struggle below the poverty line to maintain the family. This illustrates the vulnerability of some partners. The biggest challenge facing couples is not always within the dynamics of the relationship. As I have just illustrated, there can be a gap in the financial situation of the two partners. The person with the most money can have considerable power advantages in a divorce proceeding. Bob Dylan reminds us, 'Money doesn't talk. It screams out and drowns out the voice of others, especially the disadvantaged.'

Each person needs to ensure that they choose a partner who not only is a good interpersonal communicator but also a quality person. If we choose to marry a quality person, we can more readily sort through money issues, where children will receive their schooling and the cultural influence we believe will be most beneficial to their upbringing. Communication is the most sophisticated skill in the repertoire of people marrying. A quality person does not focus primarily on beauty, physique, wealth, success, power, fame, prosperity or assets. The quality of the communication will be consistent with the quality of the two persons communicating. Communication requires two quality persons. One person cannot carry a deficit in the others ability to communicate.

Chapter 11
BEING A MASTER OF COMPROMISE

As a psychologist I have found it important and sometimes necessary to carefully define what is meant by compromise. Many clients, patients and participants in courses believed they were good at compromise yet it was revealing to ask them what they meant by compromise. One example comes to mind. One couple revealed that they often disagreed over the best way to share their leisure time. The man was an enthusiastic supporter of an Australian Rules football team that often played on Friday nights. For his partner Friday night was a special opportunity to unwind together over a meal yarning about their jobs, any hassles in life and then watching a movie together. That arrangement worked until the birth for their first child then the subsequent loss of their baby sitter. They began to argue more heatedly about what to do on Friday nights.

Eventually they found a book entitled *You Can Both Be Winners*. It seemed to help them resolve the conflict over their Friday night relaxation. Later she confided to me that they had solved their problem. He could see his mates on Friday nights and she would re-join a group of friends that met on Thursday nights. At first she claimed they had made a successful compromise but she did not seem to be as happy as they both were originally. Both of them failed to recognize they were growing apart. The Friday night spent together sharing a meal had enabled them to raise important issues. With the so-called compromise, a new pattern emerged in their relationship. They spent less time together and less time airing their differences and expressing feelings. Their original issue was about having more time together not less time. They ended up spending less time together and eventually breaking up. What she had called a compromise was not a compromise at all.

No partner can avoid the need to compromise. They can remain profoundly different people who just need to keep building a bridge between each other rather than enlarge the gulf. There are more complex expressions of their differences to discover between them. What makes compromise so special and so important is that it needs to involve both partners equally and contribute to their increasing maturity.

For two partners to compromise, **both** need to get some of their own way:

Both need to communicate their thoughts, feelings and their preferences before they become habits of growing apart.
Both need to support each other.
Both should come to understand themselves and each other better i.e.: both can learn something about themselves and about the each other.
Both accept more responsibility.
Both retain their individuality and respect each other's boundaries.
Both increase their self valuing quotient and gain more respect for their partner.
Both value their individual differences and learn how bridging their differences may lead to greater intimacy.
Both experience less stress as peace breaks out.
Both become less absorbed in success and more concerned with growth.
Both have some of their needs met.
Both make contributions valued by their partner.

Both discover the limits of power when expressed in domination in contrast to the expanse opened up by the power to be one's true self.

Both end up winners and to some extent losers as both give and get – but that **is** compromise.

Compromise is not the only way to resolve differences and conflict; occasionally giving in may be productive. Sometimes it may help to barter. Even bribery has a brief sojourn. What gives compromise pride of place is the rich experiences that accompany it. When couples are invited to share examples of conflict they have resolved, it is clear that they sometimes fail to appreciate the differences between conflict resolution and compromise.

Sometimes couples are so convinced that following a set plan for compromise is the most mature way to resolve their differences, that they complicate their process of compromise unnecessarily. Sometimes the easiest way to resolve an argument is simply to give-in and agree to move on. This is difficult if one or both partners has developed a schema that compromise must be a complicated process – quite the contrary. A simple and generous solution to a problem does not always need an involved process.

Challenging negative schemas

We don't need to resolve every dispute or difference we encounter. On the contrary, it can help develop a more relaxed relationship between a couple if they share the experience of 'live and let live'.

The biggest challenge in a relationship is for partners to make sure they recognize those issues which are potential time bombs. Some problems need to be defused quickly to prevent them exploding.

A need for compromise can reflect an increasing openness to growth by each partner.

Belief 1: The fact that we are disagreeing more is a matter for concern that we are pulling apart.

Reality – Relationships are weakened not by increased recognition of differences between partners but a belief that it is safer to pretend that it will make things between us worse if we try to open up issues. If we neglect negative schema, they will not go away.

Belief 2: The more powerfully we were initially attracted to each other, the more secure we should constantly feel about the future of our relationship.

Reality – It is not trouble free circumstances that guarantee secure relationships. It is the couple's ability to raise issues of insecurity at an early stage.

Belief 3: Children will bond couples more strongly together.

Reality – Children need constant ongoing support which requires an ability to constantly adjust to their demands.

Chapter 12
ENJOYING OUR SEXUALITY

The time it takes to become a physically mature sexual being and capable of having a child is much shorter than the time it takes to become a psychologically mature sexual partner and an effective sex educator for our children.

George Bernard Shaw, the English Philosopher, was once asked by a woman at one of his public lectures whether he believed in God. He replied that he definitely did not. When asked why, his response was 'I can't trust anyone who would waste the vitality of youth on eighteen-year olds.' On another occasion he received a proposal of marriage from a very attractive young woman. She posed the question that he consider the potential of an offspring with his intelligence and her beauty. Shaw's response was immediate. He asked if she had thought of the other possibility – a child with his looks and her intelligence.

Shaw's reputation for both wisdom and wit illustrates two qualities necessary for us to meet the challenge of managing our sexuality – the Wisdom of Solomon and a sense of humour. The latter quality is necessary if we are to navigate our way through the challenges of our sexuality. You may rightly think the following story is a joke but it contains a sad truth.

A man booked in to see a psychologist. He was unhappy, confused and had difficulty relating with the many successive objects of his desire. He saw himself as an impotent failure and not a real man. In desperation the psychologist decided to use the Rorschach ink blot test. This involved showing the patient a series of what looked like ink blots and asking the patient what was the first thought that came into his mind. To every ink blot the patient responded that he saw two people having sex. The psychologist informed the man that his problem was a sexual one. When the patient asked how he knew, the psychologist replied that every one of his associations with each of the different ink blots was about sex. The patient replied: "That doesn't prove anything. My interest in sex has nothing to do with the ink blots. The fact is that I think of nothing else. Sex is on my mind all day long. That's why I came to see you."

The man had got to the heart of his sexual problem when he spoke of sex as being on his mind all day long. Sexuality is not just a mental function. Sexuality is a way of relating with other human beings. Sexuality also needs to be associated with the expression of emotion. Each human being can connect at three very different levels: what I think about sex, how I feel about sex and how I behave sexually need to be integrated. The challenge is to integrate these three expressions harmoniously and in a way that is respectful to the other.

A common mistaken belief is that the only way to express our sexuality fully is through sexual intercourse. This overlooks the need to involve the elements of mental and emotional intimacy in what can be a physically absorbing act. To maintain a deep and meaningful relationship, a person needs to be more than physically involved. There is a need to be a sexual being capable of combining the three levels of intimacy. To be a sexual being we need to keep learning about our sexual nature. No willingly shared expression of sexuality can be dirty. However, the way we think about it, the way we express it and the way we feel about it can be distorted or exaggerated. We need to learn to talk about our sexuality with a person we trust.

The challenge in establishing a sexual relationship is considerable when we try to explore the meaning of sexual involvement with a person about whom we know very little. It is no easier trying to establish a sexual relationship with a person about whom there is still a lot more to learn. It is important to learn how to relate confidently and non-sexually with a variety of people in our life.

The late poet and singer, Leonard Cohen, reminds us that 'there is a crack, a crack in everything, that's how the light gets in, that's how the light gets in...' The biggest challenge is when a person believes they have found a perfect partner. Another challenge can occur when one of the peer group mistakenly believes that the only way to secure a friendship is through sexual intercourse. One further issue is when someone believes that a deep and meaningful relationship is only possible through an active sexual life.

M*u*sturbators

There is a phrase made up of two words 'self' and 'abuse'. It illustrates the harm that is done to young people by the thoughtless use of language. Young people need to be informed that most people masturbate at some period in life. They also need to understand that our sexual energy has other important dimensions than release of sexual tension. Using the phrase 'self abuse' for masturbation can leave some men and women feeling shame and guilt. Masturbation is made into a problem when it is caught up in a web of **m*u*sturbation**. Albert Ellis singled out the word 'M*u*sturbator' to identify people who love telling people what they must do and what they must not do.

When you are trying to embrace and enjoy your sexuality, don't lose your sense of humour. The young man showing off his diving skills to impress the girls at the swimming pool will need a sense of humour if he happens to get an erection and has to dive quickly and close down the performance. The young woman who has sudden exposed bleeding will need a sense of humour if a five year old comments aloud 'How did you just cut yourself?' Healthy sexuality can embarrass many of us. Embarrassment is repeated in all the other aspects of teenage life — pimples, body shape, latest clothing fashions and hair styles, being selected early by a leader to be in their team or reaching puberty earlier or later than others. You need to know that some of your peers may have had very bad experiences with older teenagers or adults. This can happen within families.

I have developed a wish list for every adolescent:

> My wish for you is that you will enjoy the journey from adolescence to adulthood without guilt, shame or feeling overwhelmed by the pressures to conform to other adolescents' mores/standards. No one can rule out moments of embarrassment.
>
> My wish for you is that you will experience puberty and your sexuality gradually when you are ready, not at someone else's insistence or to feed their curiosity.
>
> My wish for you is that you will be able to explore your sexuality with a person of your choice whom you can trust as a friend.
>
> My wish for you is that your adolescence will confirm for you that sexuality is meant to be a very personal and private affair not a public spectacle emphasizing competition and performance.
>
> My wish for you is that you will discover that sexuality is not exclusively about gratifying our sexual urges but about learning to communicate one's self in a way that leads to appropriate early emotional, mental and physical intimacy.
>
> My wish for you is that your sexuality will remain a learning experience right though life.

My wish for you is that your first significant sexual experience will result from your considered judgement not merely from an urgent expression of an impulse out of control.

Finally, my wish for you is that by becoming a committed sexual partner you will grow into a loving parent to each child you bring into the world if that is what you really want and you have a partner who has a similar desire.

Speaking about the unspeakable – sexual abuse

There is a dark side to human sexuality when it leads to sexual abuse of children and teenagers by adults. This is especially true if the adults are in positions of trust and can include clergy, teachers, police officers, sports coaches and hospital staff. It can also include staff who look after vulnerable people with special needs. The offenders could be friends or members of one's own family. No matter where the abuse occurs, it is always a criminal offence with heavy penalties for the abuser. For adults to avoid speaking to young people about sexual abuse maybe of itself a form of abuse. Avoiding telling them may leave them vulnerable to abuse.

How does the sexual abuser operate? – recognizing the abuser

The adult may groom the young person by flattering them for their good looks, bribing them with money, gifts or making their victim feel special and important. Sometimes they use a form of hidden bullying. 'Who would want you in their team?' The victims can be very young children, adolescents or young adults.

The victim may take on the shame and guilt of the offender. Sometimes the victim starts thinking that 'the abuser must have seen something bad in me'. The fact is that the badness is only in the abuser. Sometimes the victim is led to believe that they were responsible because they enjoyed the attention before they understood what was happening. The truth is that the victim of sexual abuse has been tricked into the experience and the abuser is the only one responsible for the action which is a serious crime.

A good sexual relationship

The findings in this book suggest that a good sexual relationship is the product of wedding sexual pleasure into the joys, pains, satisfactions and frustrations of relating well. Without both these elements informing each other, the risk is that the relationship will lose or waste its energy. The enthusiasm which partners apply to the multiple tasks of sharing with and supporting each other need to constantly grow stronger. If a person can't make or express love in the way they share household chores, they may find themselves less interested in 'making love' or having sex in the double bed or on the patio. Partners need to keep their eyes open in all the activities they share or they may remain blind to other signals of marital satisfaction or dissatisfaction. These include facial expressions, small acts of affection, pleasant surprises, etc. On the other hand, it may prove costly to fail to notice grimaces, sighs and disenchantment. To overlook the many positive and negative cues people share with each other can be costly.

An important question for a successful sex life

'Do you express your sexuality with your eyes shut or open?' Who is more likely to want the lights left on when expressing sexuality? Is it men or women? And, what does it mean? One would expect men to want their eyes open. It is men who used to hang pictures of nude women in their work place. David Schnarch, the author of *Passionate Marriage*, has moved away from the view that fixing up relationships is the best approach to improving sex between partners.

A short focus on human sexuality occurred during the 1970s, in what became culturally known as the dawning of the Age of Aquarius. The discussion emphasized orgasm as the goal of sexual behaviour. Before long a shift to multiple orgasms became the goal. Finally, the goal moved to simultaneous orgasm. A more lasting and positive outcome was an increasing openness to the importance of female sexual fulfilment and the G Spot. There was an increasing awareness of the important role women played in sexual fulfilment of both men and women. The context in which these experiences were thought through or played out has survived as far more important than the search for the greatest source of physical pleasure. It is when the physical is not isolated from affection, respect or intimacy that humans report the greater sexual pleasure.

Chapter 13

UNDERSTANDING AND MONITORING OUR LEVEL OF STRESS

Each partner needs to recognize, understand and reduce their personal stress levels. It is not just human beings who experience stress. Metal experiences stress: the greatest challenge aeronautical engineers experienced in World War Two was not making planes faster than sound but making sure they did not explode into pieces as they passed through the sound barrier.

With human beings there is a limit to the amount of stress to which we can be subjected. We can easily recognize the expressions used to describe excessive stress: 'I am falling apart', 'I am cracking up', 'My friend had a nervous breakdown', 'The boss is losing the plot.' The path to mental and emotional health depends on our ability to monitor the level of stress we are experiencing. There are two main causes of stress in human beings. The first is a too fast a pace in a person's life style. The second is too much pressure.

When two partners decide to move in together it is not surprising that they may experience a high level of stress. The problem is that the idea of moving in together was assumed to make life easier, not more difficult. It was seen as a practical common sense move that would make life less complicated. It was seen as a move to reduce conflict, not make life more conflictual.

A further emerging problem was that partners had already developed individualistic ways of coping with stress. Some isolate themselves by listening to music through headphones. Some eat more. Some increase their consumption of alcohol. As the level of discomfort due to stress increases, some partners interpret the other person's discomfort as increasing disappointment with each partner's wellbeing. The problem with human stress is its' spiralling impact.

Severe stress leaves a person more vulnerable to new pressures or change. The level of discomfort and disappointment increases more quickly if we ignore the build-up of stress in ourselves and in our partners. This build-up of a new phenomenon of negative emotion was often not understood. Instead of sharing the emotions of hurt, failure, anxiety and depression, partners can begin to criticize each other's response to stress.

Dealing with Stress

Stress is a sensation that needs to be recognized and understood by those who experience it. There is no value in finding someone to blame. The strategies that help people deal with emotions need to be utilized. Human beings are body and soul. Both of these are our best ally in reducing stress.

Our body is talking to us all the time. It tells us what is bad for us. Stress can become a killer if we don't listen to our body and its many warnings. If we eat too much or eat too quickly, our body protests and we experience a stomach ache. If we drink too much alcohol, we lose our self-control and take silly risks. Stress is a major cause of poor health and early death. The tragedy is that stress comes to us as a friend but is treated as a nuisance.

Our soul censors our actions. If we ignore our spiritual self we can become cruel and brutal. The Dr Jekyll in us may be taken over by Mr Hyde.

To cope with stress we need to look after our body and our innermost spirit. We need to make good choices, in particular, valuing our health. We need to understand that stress is not a weakness. It is one of our strengths. It prevents us from destroying our body and closing down our spirit. Our body warns us against excesses of all kind. Those who have fought a major problem with alcohol can go months without drinking alcohol. So many have described how on another occasion they will choose to drink alcohol and the warning bell is silent. All around them socially are relatives and friends who have warning bells that sound when they drink too much alcohol. The alcoholic can descend into a binge which one day will destroy them prematurely.

When it comes to the human spirit, most people have a conscience which will give them no peace if they go beyond the pale, the boundary of what marks the decent from the indecent. We need to take stress seriously and listen to its positive message when it is gentle and kind. Here is a check list:

When you come home from work do you unwind with your partner?

Show affection?

Do each of you share an event from your day apart?

Do you have a ritual?

Change your clothes?

Have sex?

Pat the pet?

Spend time on a hobby?

Learn the advantage of deep breathing?

Share some music?

Sensual experience with nature - the warm sun on your body?

Are you regular with meals, sleep, work, relaxation and holidays?

Another outlet for treating stress is social action and involvement to create a gentle world – remembering that the alternative to a gentle world is a harsh world constantly calling on us to strive and acquire more. When people believe that their lives have changed for the worst, their stress level increases. When they begin to feel pressured to change, their stress level doubles. Instead of dealing with emotions of confusion, hurt, disappointment, anxiety and possibly traces of depression that have not previously surfaced, they may begin to criticize the other person's negative behaviour. Research by Gottman makes it clear that criticism of each other by both partners is an almost certain path to divorce and bitter settlements over children.

Unfortunately, many people are not taught how to manage feelings. This is dealt with in Chapter 6. We need to learn that sensations of stress need to be brought out into the open and talked about. There is an important discovery waiting to be made. Stress is not our enemy. It is an honest friend whose role, unlike advertising, is to tell us the truth.

Our body is trying to talk to us all the time. It is trying to tell us what is good for us and what is bad for us. Stress can become a killer if we ignore it. Our heart can tell us what is good for it and what is bad for it. Instead of sharing their emotions of confusion, hurt, disappointment and grief which are beginning to surface, partners risk entering a slippery slope to anxiety or depression. Alternatively, they may try to solve their problems by focusing on each other's negative behaviours and enter the blame game. Gottman's research listed criticism by partners of each other as a major cause of relationship breakdown. It is important to keep the door open to listening to and discussing the stress in each other's lives. This helps re-build stressed relationships.

Medicine is becoming as concerned with a 'bleeding heart' as a damaged aorta. Doctors are becoming more attentive to choked up emotions before prescribing medication. Psychologists are learning to respond more effectively to doctors' referrals and the experience behind them. Doctors are more concerned listening to a heartfelt story than just taking our pulse and heartbeat.

Our body and our innermost self is talking to us constantly. We can understand stress if we make friends with our body and recognize when it is speaking to us. The key to reducing stress is a healthy lifestyle. It was once summed up as eight hours work, eight hours family and play and eight hours rest. The purpose of this book is to help readers face the challenge of moderation, balance and integration in our lives. Too much emphasis on avoiding stress can make us anxious neurotics. Too much emphasis on a healthy lifestyle can leave us exhausted with endless health rituals.

We should not remove all stress from our lives. There is an optimal level of stress that we need to recognize in our lives. Without any stress we could easily become another statistic on a busy road. A too casual attitude to exams may leave us disadvantaged later in life's choice of career.

In conclusion, the goal is to make friends with our body and soul as most eloquent allies concerned for our well-being.

Chapter 14

CAREFULLY CHOOSING OUR PARTNER TO MARRY

In writing a book about marrying, it is easy for me to give an impression that I know something that the serious reader does not know but needs to know, especially when it comes to choosing a partner to marry. No matter how learned or experienced professional outsiders or our family might be, they cannot make a better choice of partner than the two people choosing to marry. My experience and philosophy is that the two partners are the ones who know deep down what is necessary for them to marry successfully.

The advice that follows is intended to set people thinking more freely. The goal is to remind the reader that what needs to find expression through marrying is something deep within both partners. This requires an erudite knowledge of one another. To this end a contemporary style dowry is a concept worth exploring. Both partners could consider giving a dowry to each other. It could be presented as a sign of deeper commitment than the customary vows. The boundaries of such a dowry would go beyond money, property and material possession to the deeply personal.

A dowry needs to touch the heart and mind of both partners receiving them. The dowry is a gift which says to the receiver I know what you really value and what delights you rather than saying it has cost me a lot of money. A gift touches the heart and mind of a partner when it leaves them feeling understood and accepted. . The best dowry would affirm to the receiver that they are understood for who they really are and would have evidence that both the giver and receiver have a capacity to keep growing an authentic self through marrying. When partners can convince each other they are able to listen in depth to each other, they know they are being taken seriously. A gift that reinforces that belief that two people have the capacity to understand each other's authentic self is invaluable.

Today couples are becoming more selective in choosing a marriage partner. Many couples include a period of living together prior to marriage. This alone does not guarantee a more realistic choice but it can help couples to reveal the sort of person they really are and want to become. It also increases the opportunity to discover and decide whether the other person is the type of person they would want to parent their children. Cohabitation can also help couples decide whether they themselves have the 'seed' qualities to cope with the realities of being a partner, a parent and a builder of community. It is true that cohabitation can be exploited and that women are more likely to be disadvantaged. Such a behaviour maybe a red alert.

The important quality for any successful partner is their ability to express their 'authentic self' in a committed loyal relationship. People are authentic when their choices are based on being the person they really are. We are talking here about a freedom which can be quite frightening, especially to those who are conservative by nature. There is a potential for tyranny if one or both partners interpret this freedom as a license to dominate their partners and their children or show early traces of narcissism or ego mania.

We need to practice judging the actions of people before we make a serious commitment to them, such as marrying. We need to be good judges of character. Carefully choosing a partner to marry can become a double-edged sword. The reasons a person may conclude that their present partner is not a good choice to marry may lead to a realization that I myself, by the same measure, am not a good choice.

Both parties have a responsibility to carefully choose their future partner

Marrying is the most complex behaviour required of people. It can shift backward and forward from infatuation to irritation, from involvement to detachment. Resolving these emotions calls for a balance of careful choices. Perhaps a longer period of getting to know each other needs to be considered. It may be undisciplined and wasteful to dismiss whatever **action love** they have shared because of self doubt. They may well need to focus, not just on solving problems they are experiencing, but on the countless times they have action loved. If partners have a history of making good choices, they are likely to have a history of distinguishing 'sober reality' from 'romantic reality' and 'harsh reality'.

'Sober reality' is a phenomenon we all need to deal with. The fact is that no matter how much effort we put into making wise choices, we cannot bend reality to our own will. Good marrying choices cannot always maintain or reproduce the joy and pleasure of an initial attraction. The realist in us appreciates this truth in the common expression that 'whether we marry, or not, we will in some ways live to regret it'. The 'sober reality' is that the most that life and marrying can offer is the opportunity to be reasonably happy for sixty percent of our lives.

'Sober reality' can help us cope with the pain of parenthood when a small child's sweetest smile can melt our heart and a moment later they can show us a disdain because we won't give them another treat. The toughest 'Sober reality' is the fact that 'life is neither fair nor just' and that the home which is meant to be the safest place can be the most dangerous.

Making good choices requires us to distinguish two sets of differences between partners. There are those which provide the ore from which couples mine the gold in their relationships. The far more difficult set of differences are those which reveal incompatibility. These differences can quickly sabotage the growth of a relationship and any attempt to enable people to marry successfully. Differences which are associated with a refusal to adjust to each other's fixed points of view will sabotage the hard won achievements of action love. A view that I will lose something of my identity if I don't get my way, is a distortion of relating well.

The goal of marrying is not focused on victory. Success is the product of learning to recognize the important elements of an alternative point of view. An ability to recognize how important that alternative view is to my partner, increases the possibility of my growth. Another important component of making good choices is the capacity to delay gratification. If I mistakenly believe that delaying gratification is a sign of weakness, I will end up stuck in my original position.

Success in marrying is strongly related to making wise choices. The person who is able to take a lead in the process of choosing wisely makes a valued partner. The condition for improving attachment is to be open to understanding why the other person is so attached to their viewpoint rather than trying to put down their view point. To understand another person's point of view, I do not have to agree with it. The reason that the ability to make wise choices is so important to marrying successfully is because it expresses respect for the other partner's point of view. Respect is an essential element in acknowledging that I value my partner. Respect is another example of action love. Lack of respect can sabotage the growing unity of two people.

There is no evidence to support the view that there are some distinctive qualities, as opposed to functions, which are exclusive to female gender and vice versa. The argument that this is the reason marriage requires a person of each gender is based on a nonsense. The fourteen qualities outlined in these chapters have no gender bias. They are not reserved for either gender. The belief that certain qualities are more commonly male attributes and certain other qualities are more commonly female attributes also has no basis other than social conditioning.

People considering such important questions as 'who to marry', 'when to marry' and 'whether to marry', need to uncover the basic essential skill in making good choices. Professor Walter Mischel from Stanford University conducted what has become known as the Marshmallow Experiment. The subjects were four to five year old children, each alone in their own room. The researcher told each child that he was leaving them in the room alone for fifteen minutes. He told each child that there was one marshmallow on their desk. If the child didn't eat the marshmallow, he/she would be rewarded with a second one as well as the first. Each child's psychological progress was tested for over forty years. The children who delayed gratification ended up with higher Scholastic Aptitude Test scores (SATS), lower levels of substance abuse and a lower likelihood of obesity. The conclusion was that young people who delayed gratification consistently achieved higher scores on a range of quality of life measures.

The importance of the Marshmallow experiment is the evidence it provided; young children can be trained early in life to acquire habits of thinking conducive to making good choices. These habits of thinking can persist throughout life. It is important to find ways to incorporate these lines of thinking in such areas as preparing to marry.

The child's ability to delay gratification and to display self-control was not a pre-determined trait. We do need to make sure that we don't inflate the meaning of these small but powerful pieces of data but, it does offer a future direction of hope for increasing the role of training the brain. The results are consistent with the work of Norman Doidge in *The Brain That Changes Itself*. It means we can train people to think positively about the benefits of marrying and encourage useful behaviour. This process needs to begin as soon as adolescents move into the broader expanse of adolescent thinking and others exclusive to those of male gender.

A far more difficult problem is incompatibility. This can occur in so many areas of marrying. This includes expectations, needs, sexuality, interests and values. One person wants to travel the world before starting their family while the other wants to start a family now while they are young. One is very attached to her family, the other finds the in-laws are a 'turn off'. These issues are more than an inability to adjust. They may be an expression of a deeper problem, an inability to risk attachment.

'Marital Tremors' are often a warning sign that people are drifting apart to avoid facing up to problems. To ignore all such warning is to risk a full marital quake or break up. A difficult choice is discerning which of these tremors needs to be acted on. Not every hiccup is a sign that partners cannot find a way to marry successfully. Marrying flourishes when our marrying choices are related more and more to sober reality and less and less on romantic reality. Partners need to edge themselves closer to sober reality.

An important question connected to choosing a partner to marry is where is the best place to initiate a relationship? The answer is often either where we work or through extended family and friendship networks.

The skill that matters most when choosing to marry is to select an environment where people can display a variety of relationship skills, social skills, attitudes and values. These are the best points of entry to developing and growing a more serious relationship. Where people work provides the most varied and realistic exposure of who they are, both their positive qualities and their limitations. In the long run it is not the most wonderful person that proves to be the best partner. The best partner to marry may be the one who is the most real, down to earth, has a sense of humour, will age gracefully and occasionally gets on your goat.

Three Important Reading Lists

Reading List 1: The challenge of being 'meaning makers', revealing ones true self and achieving intimacy thru marrying.

This is far more important than attempting to scientifically compare and contrast various marriage styles to reduce the chance of divorce. It is far more important to help partners discover what helps them marry successfully.

Frankl, Viktor E, *The Doctor of the Soul*, 1955, Vintage.
Frankl, Viktor E, *Man's Search for Meaning*, 1955, Pocket Books New York.
Frankl, Viktor E, *Psychotherapy & Existentialism*, 1967, Penguin Selected Papers.
Frankl, Viktor E, *The Will to Meaning*, 1969, Plume Books.
Kegan, Robert, *In Over Our Heads – The Mental Demands of Modern Life*, 1994, Harvard University Press London.
Kegan, Roberts, *The Evolving Self – Problems and Process In Human Development*, 1982, Harvard University Press London.

Reading List 2: The challenge of marriage.

Gottman's approach seeks a scientific and evidence based approach to marriage education.

Gottman, John M, *The Marriage Clinic*, 1999, Norton, New York.

Reading List 3: The challenge of marrying.

The following authors were able to draw attention to the pulse of our lives, the complexity of our relationships and keep us away from simplistic analyses of human intimacy and love as marrying partners. The Relatewell model has succeeded in challenging couples to recognize the value of exploring their own experiences in marrying and encouraging people to open up and share their experiences.

Buber Martin, *I And Thou*, 1923.
Burnard, Don, *Whither Now or Wither Later*, Occasional Papers, 1986, Family Relationships Institute Melbourne.

Comfort, Dr Alex, *The Joy Of Sex*, 1972, Crown Publishing Group.
Doidge, Norman, *The Brain that Changes Itself: stories of personal triumph from the frontoers of brain science*, Vicking, New York, 2007.
Dowrick, Stefanie, *Forgiveness and Other Acts Of Love*, 1997.
Fromm, Erich, *Man for Himself*, 1947, Fawcett Publications Greenwich Great Britain.
Fromm, Erich, *Escape from Freedom*, 1975.
Fromm, Erich, *The Art of Loving*, Unwin Book Great Britain.
Glasser, William, *Control Theory*, 1984, Harper and Row New York.
Goleman, Daniel, *Working with Emotional Intelligence*, 1998, Bloomsbury London.
Gottman, John M, and Nan Silver, 'How I predict divorce', *The Seven Principles for Making Marriages Work*, New York, Three Rivers Press, 1999.
Lyotard, Jean-Francois, *The Postmodern Condition*, 1979.
Marshall, Alan, writer
Masterton, James F, *The Search For The Real Self*, 1990, The Free Press New York.
May, Rollo, *Power And Innocence*, 1972, W W Norton New York.
May, Rollo, *Love And Will*, 1969, W W Norton New York.
Mischel, Walter, *The Marshmallow Test: Matering Self-Control*, Stanford University.
Rogers, Carl, *On Becoming A Person*, 1961, Constable.
Real, Terence, *Family Therapist*, 2012.
Salinger, J D, *The Catcher in the Rye*, 1951.
Saul, John Ralston,
Schnarch, David, *Passionate Marriage*, 1997, Scribe Publications Melbourne.
Seligman, Martin E P, *Learned Optimism*, 1991.
White, Michael, *Reauthoring Lives*, 1995, Dulwich Centre South Australia.

MARRYING

www.ingramcontent.com/pod-product-compliance
Lightning Source LLC
Chambersburg PA
CBHW050556300426
44112CB00013B/1948